DEEP LEARNING IN HEALTHCARE: UNLOCKING THE POTENTIAL OF MEDICAL DATA

S.FOWJIYA

Contents

1. INTRODUCTION — 1

2. THE DATA DELUGE IN HEALTHCARE — 4

3. A TRESURE TROVE OF VISUAL INFORMATION — 25

4. RISE OF DEEP LEARNING — 43

5. DEEP LEARNING'S IMPACT ON MEDICAL IMAGING — 51

6. BEYOND IMAGES: DEEP LEARNING'S DIVERSE APPLICATIONS — 57

7. CHALLENGES AND CONSIDERATIONS — 69

8. DEEP LEARNING EMPOWERING R&D — 85

9. DEEP LEARNING AND PATIENT ENGAGEMENT — 96

10. DEEP LEARNING IN ACTION: REAL-WORLD EXAMPLES — 106

11. CONCLUSION — 114

12. REFERENCES — 117

13. ABOUT AUTHORS — 120

CHAPTER ONE

INTRODUCTION

The healthcare industry stands at the precipice of a revolution. Fueled by the transformative power of deep learning, a sophisticated form of artificial intelligence (AI), vast amounts of medical data are being unlocked to unlock a new era of healthcare. This data, once a silent observer, is now poised to become a powerful force for good, offering a multitude of benefits for patients, healthcare providers, and the future of medicine itself.

This report delves into how deep learning is transforming healthcare by:

- **Revolutionizing Clinical Trials:** Deep learning can optimize clinical trial design, accelerating the development of life-saving treatments.
- **Empowering Personalized Medicine:** By analyzing an individual's unique genetic makeup, health data, and real-time information, deep learning personalizes medicine, leading to tailored preventive measures, more effective treatments, and improved patient outcomes.
- **Transforming Patient Engagement:** Virtual assistants and chatbots powered by deep learning empower patients by providing 24/7 access to information, appointment scheduling tools, and personalized

guidance, fostering a more proactive approach to health management.

- **Enhancing Remote Monitoring:** Wearable devices and remote monitoring platforms powered by deep learning allow healthcare professionals to continuously track patient health data outside the clinical setting, enabling early disease detection, improved disease management, and empowering patients to take charge of their health.

- **Personalized Health Risk Assessment:** Deep learning personalizes health risk assessments by incorporating a wider range of factors and vast datasets, allowing for early identification of potential health risks and promoting a future of proactive healthcare.

- **Early Disease Detection:** Advancements like DeepMind's AI for diabetic retinopathy detection and Freenome's multiomics platform for early cancer screening exemplify how deep learning is revolutionizing disease detection with the potential to save lives through earlier intervention.

- **Empowering Healthcare Professionals:** Enlitic's AI platform for medical image analysis is a prime example of how deep learning assists healthcare professionals. By streamlining workflows, enhancing diagnostic accuracy, and facilitating research, AI empowers them to deliver better care.

While the potential of deep learning in healthcare is vast, challenges remain. These include ensuring data privacy and security, navigating regulatory hurdles, mitigating algorithmic bias, and ensuring equitable access to these technologies. Addressing these challenges and fostering responsible development are crucial to ensuring deep learning fulfills its transformative promise.

This report concludes by exploring the exciting possibilities that lie ahead – a future where deep learning unlocks the full potential of medical data, ushering in an era of personalized, data-driven medicine. Imagine a future where preventive measures are tailored to your unique needs, treatments are optimized for your specific biology, and you are empowered to actively participate in your own health journey. This is the future that deep learning in healthcare promises to create.

CHAPTER TWO

THE DATA DELUGE IN HEALTHCARE

The healthcare industry is experiencing a data explosion unlike anything ever seen before. This phenomenon, often referred to as the "data deluge," is fueled by several factors:

Electronic Health Records (EHRs): The healthcare industry has undergone a revolution with the widespread adoption of Electronic Health Records (EHRs). These digital systems have replaced the cumbersome paper charts of the past, leading to a gargantuan increase in the amount of data captured about patients. EHRs are no longer limited to basic demographics. They now encompass a rich tapestry of information, including:

- **Clinical Encounters:** Detailed doctors' notes, diagnoses, treatment plans, and progress reports.
- **Diagnostic Data:** Lab results, radiology reports, pathology findings, and other diagnostic tests.
- **Medication Management:** Comprehensive medication history, current prescriptions, allergies, and potential drug interactions.
- **Imaging Data:** X-rays, MRIs, CT scans, and other visual representations of a patient's internal health.

- **Preventive Care:** Vaccination records, screening results, and reminders for upcoming wellness checks.
- **Social Determinants of Health:** Information about a patient's socioeconomic status, living environment, and access to healthcare resources.

This data deluge presents a double-edged sword.
Benefits:

- **Improved Care Coordination:** With a complete medical history readily accessible, doctors can make more informed treatment decisions, avoiding unnecessary tests and medications.
- **Enhanced Research:** The vast trove of anonymized patient data can fuel groundbreaking research in disease prevention, treatment optimization, and personalized medicine.
- **Streamlined Workflows:** EHRs automate tasks like appointment scheduling, medication refills, and lab report retrieval, freeing up valuable time for patient interaction.
- **Population Health Management:** Analyzing large datasets helps identify trends in disease prevalence and risk factors, allowing healthcare systems to focus preventive efforts on high-risk populations.

Challenges:

- **Data Security and Privacy:** Safeguarding sensitive patient information is paramount. Robust cybersecurity measures and strict adherence to privacy regulations like HIPAA are crucial.

- **Data Interoperability:** Different EHR systems may not communicate seamlessly, hindering information sharing between healthcare providers.
- **Data Overload:** Clinicians can be overwhelmed by the sheer volume of data, making it difficult to identify the most relevant information for patient care.
- **Clinician Burnout:** The time spent navigating complex EHR systems can detract from face-to-face patient interaction, potentially leading to clinician burnout.

The future of healthcare hinges on harnessing the power of EHR data while mitigating the challenges. By developing user-friendly interfaces, fostering data interoperability, and investing in robust data security, we can unlock the full potential of this digital revolution for the benefit of patients and healthcare professionals alike.

Demographic Information: Demographic information is a crucial component of EHR data. It forms the foundation for understanding a patient's background and potential health risks. Here's a breakdown of some key demographic elements captured in EHRs:

- **Essential Demographics:**

  - Age: This is critical for tailoring treatment plans and understanding age-related health risks.
  - Sex/Gender: Influences disease presentation, medication selection, and preventive screening needs.
  - Race and Ethnicity: Can influence disease prevalence and response to treatment.

- **Family History:**

- Documents genetic predispositions to certain diseases like cancer, heart disease, or mental health conditions.

- **Social Determinants of Health (SDoH):**

  - This is a growing area of focus. It captures information about a patient's socioeconomic status, living environment, access to healthcare, and education level. These factors significantly impact health outcomes.

Clinical Encounters: Clinical encounters are a cornerstone of EHR data, capturing the dynamic back-and-forth between a healthcare provider and patient. Here's a deeper dive into what this entails:
Content of Clinical Encounters:

- **Doctors' Notes:** These detailed narratives document the physician's observations, assessments, thought processes, and clinical reasoning during a patient visit.
- **Diagnoses:** Confirmed or suspected conditions based on clinical findings, lab results, and imaging data. It can include primary and secondary diagnoses.
- **Treatment Plans:** Strategies outlined to address the patient's medical concerns. This may involve medications, procedures, therapies, referrals to specialists, and patient education.
- **Medication Orders:** Specific medications prescribed, dosages, and instructions for use. This section also often includes documentation of allergies and medication reconciliation (reviewing all medications the patient is taking to avoid duplicates or interactions).

- **Progress Notes:** These document the patient's response to treatment and any changes made to the plan over time.

Significance of Clinical Encounters:

- **Continuity of Care:** Provides a chronological record of a patient's interaction with the healthcare system, enabling informed decision-making for subsequent healthcare providers.
- **Quality Improvement:** Allows for monitoring and evaluation of treatment effectiveness, helping to identify areas for improvement in patient care.
- **Billing and Coding:** Supports accurate medical billing based on the services provided during the encounter.

Challenges and Considerations:

- **Note Quality and Standardization:** The quality and completeness of doctors' notes can vary depending on the physician and available time. Efforts are underway to standardize note-taking to improve clarity and efficiency.
- **Time Constraints:** Clinicians may feel pressure to rush through documentation, potentially impacting the detail captured in clinical encounters.
- **Patient Engagement:** Integrating patient narratives and self-reported information into clinical encounters can provide a more holistic view of their health.

Clinical encounter data is a rich resource for understanding patient care delivery and improving healthcare outcomes. By addressing existing challenges and promoting best practices in documentation, we can unlock its full potential.

Laboratory Results: Laboratory results are a goldmine of information within EHR data, offering a window into a patient's internal health. Let's delve deeper into the different types of laboratory results captured in EHRs:

1. Blood Tests: These are the workhorses of laboratory diagnostics, analyzing the composition and function of blood. Common blood tests include:

- **Complete Blood Count (CBC):** Measures the number and types of red and white blood cells, platelets, and hemoglobin (oxygen-carrying protein in red blood cells). It can indicate infections, anemia, and other blood disorders.
- **Chemistry Panels:** Evaluate various organ functions by measuring levels of electrolytes, enzymes, proteins, and other substances in the blood. They can help diagnose problems with the liver, kidneys, heart, and other organs.
- **Hormone Tests:** Assess the levels of hormones produced by different glands in the body, helping diagnose hormonal imbalances related to thyroid function, fertility, diabetes, and more.
- **Blood Culture:** Used to detect bacteria or fungi in the bloodstream, helping diagnose infections like sepsis.
- **Lipid Panel:** Measures cholesterol levels (LDL, HDL, and triglycerides) to assess cardiovascular disease risk.

2. Imaging Reports: These visual representations provide crucial insights into internal structures:

- **X-rays:** Capture images of bones and joints, aiding in diagnosing fractures, arthritis, and other bone abnormalities.
- **Magnetic Resonance Imaging (MRI):** Creates detailed images of organs, soft tissues, and bones using powerful magnets and radio waves. It's helpful for diagnosing tumors, injuries, and neurological conditions.
- **Computed Tomography (CT) Scans:** Combine multiple X-ray images to create detailed cross-sectional views of the body, providing a more comprehensive picture of internal structures than X-rays alone.

3. Pathology Findings: Microscopic examination of tissues or fluids plays a vital role in diagnosing diseases:

- **Biopsies:** Removal and examination of a small sample of tissue to diagnose cancer, infections, and other conditions.
- **Cytology:** Microscopic examination of cells from various body fluids (e.g., pap smears) to detect abnormalities suggestive of cancer or precancerous conditions.

By integrating these diverse laboratory results into EHRs, healthcare professionals gain a more comprehensive understanding of a patient's health. This information is crucial for:

- **Accurate Diagnosis:** Laboratory results help confirm or rule out suspected conditions.
- **Monitoring Treatment Effectiveness:** Tracking changes in lab values over time allows doctors to assess how well a treatment is working.

- **Early Detection of Disease:** Certain lab abnormalities can indicate an increased risk for future health problems, prompting preventive measures.

However, challenges exist with laboratory results in EHRs:

- **Standardization:** Variation in test names, reference ranges, and reporting formats across labs can complicate data interpretation.
- **Turnaround Time:** Delays in receiving results can hinder timely clinical decisions.
- **Patient Education:** Understanding complex lab results can be challenging for patients. Clear explanations and patient portals can empower informed healthcare decisions.

By addressing these challenges and promoting data standardization, laboratories can play a vital role in optimizing the use of EHR data for improved patient care.

Immunization Records: Immunization records are a crucial component of EHR data, acting as a vital log of a patient's vaccination history. Here's a closer look at the information captured in these records:

- **Vaccine Types:** This details all the vaccinations a patient has received, including:

  - Measles, Mumps, and Rubella (MMR)
  - Diphtheria, Tetanus, and Pertussis (DTaP)
  - Polio
  - Varicella (chickenpox)
  - Human Papillomavirus (HPV)

- Influenza (flu)
- Pneumococcal (pneumonia)
- Meningococcal (meningitis)
- And many others depending on age, health conditions, and travel history.

- **Vaccination Dates:** Records the exact date each vaccine was administered. This ensures patients stay on schedule for recommended immunization intervals.
- **Dosage:** Documents the amount of vaccine administered, ensuring proper protection.
- **Lot Numbers:** Tracks the specific batch of vaccine used, facilitating identification and potential recall if necessary.
- **Provider Information:** Records the healthcare provider who administered the vaccination.
- **Side Effects:** Documents any adverse reactions a patient may have experienced after receiving a vaccine.

Significance of Immunization Records:

- **Disease Prevention:** Immunization records are essential for maintaining herd immunity and preventing outbreaks of infectious diseases. By tracking vaccination rates, public health officials can identify areas where immunization efforts need to be focused.
- **Personalized Vaccination Schedules:** They ensure patients receive appropriate vaccinations at the recommended intervals based on their age and health conditions. This helps prevent vaccine-preventable illnesses.
- **Improved Public Health Outcomes:** Tracking vaccination coverage rates and identifying disease

trends allows for targeted public health interventions and resource allocation.

Challenges of Immunization Records:

- **Incomplete Records:** Missing or outdated information can hinder ensuring patients are up-to-date on vaccinations. This can occur due to:

  - Lack of data exchange between healthcare providers
  - Patients receiving vaccinations outside traditional healthcare settings (e.g., travel clinics, pharmacies)
  - Reliance on patient recall

- **Data Sharing:** Limited data exchange between healthcare providers can lead to incomplete records. This can be due to:

  - Incompatible EHR systems
  - Privacy concerns

Overcoming Challenges:

- **Standardized Immunization Information Systems:** Implementing standardized systems for recording and sharing immunization data across different healthcare providers ensures complete and accurate records.
- **Patient Portals:** Providing patients with access to their immunization records through online portals empowers them to track their vaccination status and share it with healthcare providers as needed.
- **Immunization Reminders:** EHR systems can generate automatic reminders for upcoming vaccinations,

prompting patients to stay on schedule.

By addressing these challenges and promoting data exchange, immunization records can be a powerful tool for promoting public health and ensuring individual well-being.

Medication History: Medication history is a critical component of EHR data, acting as a central hub for information on a patient's current medications and past interactions with drugs. Let's delve deeper into the details captured in medication history within EHRs:

Information Included:

- **Current Prescriptions:** A detailed list of all medications a patient is currently taking, including:

  - Generic and brand names
  - Dosages and frequencies
  - Routes of administration (e.g., oral, topical, injection)
  - Start and end dates of prescriptions (if applicable)

- **Over-the-Counter Medications:** While not always captured comprehensively, some EHRs allow documenting any over-the-counter medications or supplements a patient is taking.
- **Medication Allergies:** A list of any allergies a patient has to specific medications or drug classes. This is crucial for preventing potentially life-threatening allergic reactions.
- **Adverse Drug Reactions:** Documentation of any negative side effects a patient has experienced from medications. This information helps healthcare

providers avoid prescribing medications that may cause similar reactions.

Significance of Medication History:

- **Improved Medication Safety:** Having a complete medication history allows healthcare providers to:

  - Identify and avoid potential drug interactions
  - Prevent prescribing medications a patient is allergic to
  - Ensure appropriate dosages for a patient's age, weight, and kidney or liver function

- **Enhanced Treatment Planning:** Knowing a patient's medication history helps providers tailor treatment plans to avoid conflicts with existing medications.
- **Medication Adherence Monitoring:** By tracking refills and reviewing medication lists, healthcare professionals can assess a patient's adherence to prescribed medications.

Challenges of Medication History:

- **Accuracy and Completeness:** Reliance on patient recall and self-reported information can lead to inaccuracies.
- **Data Sharing:** Limited data exchange between healthcare providers (e.g., pharmacies, hospitals, specialists) can result in incomplete medication histories.
- **Lack of Standardization:** Variations in medication names and coding across different systems can create confusion.

Overcoming Challenges:

- **Patient Engagement:** Encouraging patients to maintain a medication log and share information about all medications they are taking can improve accuracy.
- **Improved Data Sharing:** Standardizing medication information formats and fostering better data exchange between healthcare providers ensures comprehensive medication histories.
- **EHR Integration with Pharmacies:** Integrating EHR systems with pharmacies allows for automatic updates on dispensed medications, improving medication list accuracy.

By addressing these challenges and promoting patient engagement, medication history data within EHRs can become a powerful tool for ensuring medication safety, optimizing treatment plans, and improving patient outcomes.

Progress Notes: Progress notes are the lifeblood of documenting a patient's journey within an EHR system. They offer a chronological narrative of a patient's condition, treatment response, and overall health status over time. Here's a breakdown of what progress notes capture:

Content of Progress Notes:

- **Subjective:** This section captures the patient's perspective on their health. It may include their symptoms, concerns, and self-reported experiences since the last visit.
- **Objective:** Here, the healthcare provider documents their observations during the encounter. This may

include vital signs, physical examination findings, and test results.

- **Assessment:** This section is the healthcare professional's analysis of the patient's condition. They interpret the subjective and objective data to arrive at a diagnosis or working diagnosis.
- **Plan:** This outlines the course of action for the patient's care. It may include medication adjustments, referral to specialists, additional testing, or recommendations for lifestyle modifications.

Significance of Progress Notes:

- **Continuity of Care:** Progress notes create a detailed record of a patient's interaction with the healthcare system, enabling informed decision-making by subsequent healthcare providers involved in the patient's care.
- **Monitoring Treatment Effectiveness:** By tracking changes in a patient's condition over time, progress notes allow healthcare professionals to assess the effectiveness of treatment plans and make necessary adjustments.
- **Quality Improvement:** Progress notes can be used to evaluate the quality of care provided by analyzing trends and identifying areas for improvement in patient care delivery.
- **Medico-legal Documentation:** Progress notes serve as legal documentation of a patient's care, protecting both the patient and the healthcare provider.

Challenges of Progress Notes:

- **Time Constraints:** Clinicians may feel pressured to rush through documentation, potentially impacting the detail captured in progress notes.
- **Note Quality and Standardization:** The quality and completeness of progress notes can vary depending on the physician's writing style and available time. Efforts are underway to standardize note-taking through templates or problem-oriented medical record (POMR) systems, which improve clarity and efficiency.
- **Data Overload:** With extensive progress notes accumulating over time, it can be challenging for healthcare professionals to identify the most relevant information for decision-making. Advanced data visualization tools can help navigate this data overload.

The Future of Progress Notes:

- **Integration with Clinical Decision Support Systems:** EHRs can integrate with clinical decision support systems (CDSS) that prompt healthcare providers with relevant questions or suggestions based on progress note content, potentially improving decision-making.
- **Speech Recognition Technology:** Speech recognition technology can streamline progress note creation, reducing documentation burden on clinicians.
- **Patient Engagement:** Integrating patient narratives and self-reported information into progress notes can provide a more holistic view of their health and empower shared decision-making.

By addressing existing challenges and embracing new technologies, progress notes can evolve to become even more powerful tools for optimizing patient care and ensuring continuity of care within the EHR system.

- This wealth of data offers a multitude of benefits for patients, healthcare providers, and the healthcare system as a whole:

Enhanced Patient Care:

- **Improved Continuity of Care:** EHRs provide a centralized, accessible record of a patient's medical history, allowing healthcare providers to gain a more comprehensive understanding of their patients' conditions and treatment history. This can lead to improved quality of care, reduced medication errors, and better-informed treatment decisions.
- **More Effective Care Coordination:** EHRs facilitate communication and collaboration between different healthcare providers involved in a patient's care. This can lead to a more coordinated approach to treatment, reducing duplication of services and improving overall patient outcomes.
- **Empowerment and Patient Engagement:** EHR systems can provide patients with secure online access to their medical records. This allows patients to be more actively involved in their own healthcare decisions, manage their medications effectively, and track their health progress over time.

Benefits for Healthcare Providers:

- **Increased Efficiency:** EHRs streamline workflows by automating tasks like prescription writing, lab order entry, and charting. This frees up valuable time for clinicians to focus on patient interaction and provide better care.

- **Improved Decision-Making:** EHRs provide a wealth of data that can be used to support evidence-based medicine. Clinicians can leverage this data to make more informed treatment decisions and improve patient outcomes.
- **Enhanced Research Opportunities:** The vast amount of anonymized patient data stored in EHRs can be a valuable resource for medical research. Researchers can utilize this data to identify trends, develop new treatments, and improve overall healthcare knowledge.

Transforming the Healthcare System:

- **Reduced Costs:** Improved care coordination and reduced duplication of services can lead to cost savings for the healthcare system.
- **Public Health Monitoring:** EHR data can be aggregated and analyzed to track disease outbreaks, identify emerging public health threats, and inform public health interventions.
- **Improved Quality Metrics:** EHRs can be used to track and measure healthcare quality metrics, allowing healthcare providers and institutions to identify areas for improvement and benchmark performance.

However, the EHR revolution is not without its challenges:

- **Data Security and Privacy:** Ensuring the security and privacy of sensitive patient data stored in EHRs is paramount. Robust cybersecurity measures and clear data governance practices are crucial.

- **Interoperability Challenges:** Different EHR systems may not communicate seamlessly with each other, hindering data exchange and creating roadblocks to efficient care coordination.
- **Implementation Costs:** The initial costs of implementing and maintaining EHR systems can be significant, especially for smaller healthcare providers.
- **Usability and Workflow Integration:** Clinician burnout can be exacerbated by poorly designed EHR systems that disrupt workflows and hinder efficiency.

Despite these challenges, the potential benefits of EHRs are undeniable. As the technology continues to evolve and challenges are addressed, EHRs are poised to play a central role in shaping the future of healthcare, fostering a future of improved patient care, efficient healthcare delivery, and groundbreaking medical discoveries.

Medical Imaging: Medical imaging has become a cornerstone of modern medicine, offering invaluable insights into the human body. However, the technological advancements that bring us detailed MRIs, CT scans, and X-rays also create a significant challenge: storing and managing the vast amount of data these images generate. Here's a deeper look at this data deluge:

Types of Medical Imaging Data:

- **Digital Imaging and Communications in Medicine (DICOM):** This is the standard format for storing and transmitting medical images. It ensures compatibility across different imaging equipment and software.
- **Image Size:** Medical images can be very large, containing millions of pixels, leading to significant

storage requirements.

- **3D Reconstructions:** Advanced imaging techniques like MRIs and CT scans can generate 3D reconstructions of organs and tissues, further increasing data volume.

Challenges of Medical Imaging Data Storage:

- **Storage Capacity:** The sheer volume of imaging data can quickly strain storage capabilities of healthcare institutions.
- **Data Archiving:** Long-term storage of medical images is crucial for patient care and research purposes. However, traditional storage methods can be expensive and cumbersome.
- **Data Access and Retrieval:** Efficiently accessing and retrieving specific medical images from vast archives is essential for patient care.

Solutions for Managing Medical Imaging Data:

- **Data Compression Techniques:** Advanced compression algorithms can significantly reduce the file size of medical images without compromising diagnostic quality.
- **Cloud-Based Storage:** Cloud storage offers scalable and cost-effective solutions for storing and managing medical imaging data.
- **Data Archiving Systems:** Implementing robust data archiving systems with efficient indexing and retrieval mechanisms ensures long-term accessibility of medical images.

The Rise of Big Data in Medical Imaging:

The vast amount of medical imaging data presents a unique opportunity for Big Data analytics. By analyzing large datasets of medical images, researchers can:

- **Develop AI-powered tools:** These tools can assist radiologists in image interpretation, potentially improving diagnostic accuracy and efficiency.
- **Identify disease patterns:** Large-scale analysis of medical images can help identify subtle patterns and trends associated with specific diseases, leading to earlier diagnoses and better treatment strategies.
- **Personalized Medicine:** Advanced image analysis can pave the way for personalized medicine by tailoring treatment plans based on individual patient characteristics visualized through medical imaging.

The Future of Medical Imaging Data Management:
As medical imaging technology continues to evolve, so too will the need for sophisticated data management solutions. By embracing cloud storage, data compression techniques, and advanced data analysis tools, healthcare institutions can unlock the full potential of medical imaging data to revolutionize healthcare delivery.

- Technological advancements have revolutionized medical imaging, ushering in a new era of diagnostic precision. Sophisticated tools like Magnetic Resonance Imaging (MRI), Computed Tomography (CT) scans, and X-rays have become commonplace, generating a wealth of visual data that plays a pivotal role in modern healthcare. However, these images present a unique challenge – the sheer volume of data they produce necessitates innovative solutions for storage and analysis.

CHAPTER THREE

A TRESURE TROVE OF VISUAL INFORMATION

Medical imaging modalities capture a wide range of internal body structures and functions, providing invaluable insights for diagnosis, treatment planning, and disease monitoring. Here's a glimpse into the types of data generated:

X-rays: These provide basic two-dimensional images of bones and some soft tissues, aiding in detecting fractures, infections, and certain abnormalities.X-rays are a workhorse of medical imaging, offering a simple yet effective way to visualize bones and some internal structures. Here's a closer look at the specific uses of X-rays:

Advantages of X-rays:

- **Fast and Readily Available:** X-rays are a relatively quick and painless procedure, making them ideal for emergency settings or when a rapid assessment is needed.

- **Cost-Effective:** Compared to more advanced imaging techniques like MRIs or CT scans, X-rays are significantly less expensive.
- **Excellent for Bones:** X-rays provide clear visualization of bones, making them ideal for diagnosing fractures, dislocations, bone tumors, and abnormalities like arthritis.
- **Certain Soft Tissues:** While primarily used for bones, X-rays can also be helpful in visualizing some soft tissues like lungs (chest X-rays) to identify pneumonia or foreign objects.

Limitations of X-rays:

- **Limited Soft Tissue Visibility:** X-rays are not ideal for visualizing most soft tissues like muscles, organs, or blood vessels.
- **Radiation Exposure:** While the radiation dose from a single X-ray is generally low, repeated X-rays can increase a patient's cumulative radiation exposure. This is a consideration, particularly for children or pregnant women.
- **Two-Dimensional Images:** X-rays provide only a flat, two-dimensional image, which may obscure details in complex anatomical structures.

When are X-rays used?

- **Fractures:** X-rays are the gold standard for diagnosing fractures in bones.
- **Joint Injuries:** They can be used to assess joint dislocations and alignment.

- **Chest Infections:** Chest X-rays can help identify pneumonia, fluid buildup in the lungs (pleural effusion), and certain lung tumors.
- **Abdominal Issues:** While limited, X-rays can sometimes be used to visualize foreign objects ingested by a patient or identify certain bowel obstructions.
- **Dental X-rays:** A specialized type of X-ray used to examine teeth, jawbone, and surrounding structures for cavities, root infections, and other dental problems.

The Role of X-rays in the EHR:
Digital X-ray images are seamlessly integrated into EHR systems, allowing healthcare providers to:

- **Review X-rays alongside other patient data** for a more comprehensive understanding of a patient's condition.
- **Track changes in X-ray images** over time to monitor treatment progress.
- **Share X-rays electronically** with specialists for consultation, improving collaboration and care coordination.

In conclusion, X-rays, despite their limitations, remain a valuable and widely used tool in medical imaging. Their simplicity, affordability, and effectiveness for visualizing bones make them a cornerstone of diagnostic procedures across various healthcare settings.

CT scans: These create detailed cross-sectional images of the body, offering a more comprehensive view of organs, bones, and blood vessels. CT scans are used for diagnosing various conditions, including cancer, heart disease, and internal injuries.CT scans, or Computed Tomography scans, have revolutionized medical imaging by providing a much more detailed view of the body's interior compared to X-rays. Let's delve deeper into the advantages and applications of CT scans:

Advantages of CT Scans:

- **Detailed Cross-Sectional Images:** CT scans generate a series of detailed cross-sectional images (slices) of the body, offering a more comprehensive view of organs, bones, soft tissues, and blood vessels compared to flat X-ray images.
- **Versatility:** CT scans can be used to image virtually any part of the body, making them valuable for diagnosing a wide range of conditions.
- **Quick and Painless:** The CT scan procedure itself is generally quick and painless, although some patients may experience slight discomfort from lying still during the scan.
- **Non-invasive:** Unlike some diagnostic procedures, CT scans are non-invasive, meaning they don't involve inserting instruments into the body.

Applications of CT Scans:

- **Cancer Diagnosis and Staging:** CT scans play a crucial role in diagnosing cancer, identifying its location, size, and spread (staging) to guide treatment planning.
- **Heart Disease Diagnosis:** CT scans can be used to assess heart function, detect coronary artery blockages, and identify abnormalities in the heart valves or aorta.
- **Internal Injuries:** In emergency situations, CT scans can help identify internal bleeding, organ damage, or fractures after an accident or trauma.

- **Musculoskeletal Conditions:** CT scans can visualize bone fractures, joint abnormalities, and assess muscle or ligament tears.
- **Neurological Conditions:** CT scans of the head can help diagnose strokes, brain tumors, and other neurological conditions.

Limitations of CT Scans:

- **Radiation Exposure:** CT scans use ionizing radiation, which carries a small risk of developing cancer, particularly with repeated scans.
- **Cost:** CT scans are generally more expensive than X-rays.
- **Not ideal for certain tissues:** While CT scans offer a good view of most tissues, they may not be the best option for visualizing some soft tissues like the brain, where MRI scans are preferred.

The Role of CT Scans in the EHR:
Similar to X-rays, CT scan images are integrated into EHR systems, enabling healthcare providers to:

- **Review CT scans alongside other patient data** for a more comprehensive picture of a patient's condition.
- **Track changes in CT scan images** over time to monitor treatment progress or disease progression.
- **Share CT scans electronically** with specialists for consultation, improving care coordination.

The Future of CT Scans:
Advancements in CT scan technology are ongoing, with a focus on:

- **Reducing radiation dose:** Newer CT scanners use lower radiation doses while maintaining image quality.
- **Faster scan times:** Technological advancements are leading to quicker scan times, reducing patient discomfort and improving workflow efficiency.
- **Advanced image analysis tools:** Integrating artificial intelligence (AI) into CT scan analysis can improve diagnostic accuracy and expedite reporting.

In conclusion, CT scans offer a powerful tool for diagnosing a wide range of medical conditions. While considerations regarding radiation exposure exist, advancements in technology are continuously improving safety and efficiency. CT scans, integrated with EHR systems, empower healthcare professionals to make more informed diagnoses and treatment decisions, ultimately leading to better patient outcomes.

MRIs: MRIs utilize powerful magnetic fields and radio waves to produce detailed images of organs, soft tissues, and the brain. MRIs are crucial for diagnosing neurological conditions, musculoskeletal injuries, and certain cancers.

Magnetic Resonance Imaging (MRI) scans offer a non-invasive window into the human body, providing unparalleled detail of organs, soft tissues, and especially the brain. Here's a closer look at what makes MRIs so valuable in the diagnostic landscape:

Advantages of MRIs:

- **Exceptional Soft Tissue Detail:** Unlike X-rays or CT scans, MRIs excel at visualizing soft tissues like muscles, ligaments, the brain, and spinal cord. This makes them ideal for diagnosing conditions affecting these structures.

- **No Ionizing Radiation:** MRIs use strong magnetic fields and radio waves to create images, eliminating the risk of radiation exposure associated with X-rays and CT scans.
- **Detailed Functional Imaging:** Certain MRI techniques can assess not only structure but also function. For example, functional MRI (fMRI) can map brain activity during tasks, aiding in neurological diagnoses.

Applications of MRIs:

- **Neurological Conditions:** MRIs are the gold standard for diagnosing neurological conditions like multiple sclerosis, tumors, strokes, and epilepsy. They provide detailed images of the brain and spinal cord, enabling precise evaluation.
- **Musculoskeletal Injuries:** MRIs can reveal ligament tears, muscle strains, and bone abnormalities in much greater detail than X-rays, aiding in treatment planning for sports injuries or other musculoskeletal problems.
- **Cancer Diagnosis:** MRIs can be used to diagnose certain cancers, particularly those affecting soft tissues or the brain, by identifying abnormalities in tissue structure.
- **Cardiovascular Imaging:** Advanced MRI techniques can assess heart function and identify abnormalities in blood vessels.

Limitations of MRIs:

- **Cost:** MRIs are generally more expensive than X-rays or CT scans.
- **Scan Time:** MRI scans can take longer than X-rays or CT scans, and some patients may experience claustrophobia within the enclosed MRI machine.

- **Metal Implants:** People with certain metal implants or claustrophobia may not be suitable candidates for MRI scans.

The Role of MRIs in EHR:

MRI images are seamlessly integrated into EHR systems, allowing healthcare providers to:

- **Review MRIs alongside other patient data** for a more comprehensive understanding of a patient's condition.
- **Track changes in MRI images** over time to monitor treatment progress or disease progression.
- **Share MRIs electronically** with specialists for consultation, improving collaboration and care coordination.

The Future of MRIs:

Advancements in MRI technology are focused on:

- **Reduced Scan Times:** Shorter scan times can improve patient comfort and workflow efficiency.
- **Improved Image Quality:** Technological improvements are continually enhancing the resolution and detail of MRI images.
- **Advanced Techniques:** New MRI techniques like diffusion tensor imaging (DTI) are providing even deeper insights into brain connectivity and function.

In conclusion, MRIs are a powerful diagnostic tool offering exceptional detail of soft tissues and the brain. While cost and scan time considerations exist, MRIs play a crucial role in diagnosing a wide range of medical conditions. When integrated with EHR systems, MRI data empowers healthcare professionals to deliver more informed diagnoses and targeted treatments, ultimately leading to improved patient care.

Ultrasound: This technology uses sound waves to generate real-time images of internal organs and soft tissues. Ultrasounds are commonly used in pregnancy monitoring and for examining the heart, abdomen, and blood flow.Ultrasound is a versatile and valuable imaging technique that utilizes sound waves to create real-time images of internal organs and soft tissues. Here's a deeper dive into the advantages, applications, and considerations of ultrasound in medical imaging:

Advantages of Ultrasound:

- **Real-Time Imaging:** Unlike X-rays, CT scans, or MRIs, ultrasound provides real-time moving images of internal structures. This allows healthcare providers to visualize organ function, blood flow, and even fetal development in real-time.
- **Painless and Non-invasive:** Ultrasound exams are painless and non-invasive. They use sound waves and don't involve radiation exposure, making them a safe option for pregnant women and children.
- **Relatively Affordable:** Compared to other imaging techniques like CT scans or MRIs, ultrasounds are generally more affordable.
- **Portable Equipment:** Ultrasound machines are often portable, allowing for examinations at the bedside or in outpatient settings.

Applications of Ultrasound:

- **Pregnancy Monitoring:** Ultrasound is the gold standard for prenatal care, allowing visualization of the fetus, monitoring its growth and development, and identifying potential complications.
- **Abdominal Imaging:** Ultrasound can be used to examine the liver, kidneys, gallbladder, pancreas, and other abdominal organs to detect abnormalities like tumors, gallstones, or fluid buildup.
- **Pelvic Imaging:** Ultrasound can assess the uterus, ovaries, and prostate gland for abnormalities like cysts, fibroids, or tumors.
- **Echocardiography:** This specialized ultrasound technique visualizes the heart, assessing its structure and function, and helping diagnose heart conditions.
- **Musculoskeletal Imaging:** Ultrasound can be used to examine muscles, tendons, and joints for tears, strains, or other injuries.

Limitations of Ultrasound:

- **Limited Tissue Penetration:** Ultrasound waves cannot penetrate deeply through bone or air, limiting their ability to image certain structures.
- **Image Quality Dependence:** The quality of ultrasound images can vary depending on the skill of the technician and the patient's body composition.
- **Operator Dependence:** Interpretation of ultrasound images requires skilled professionals trained in ultrasound techniques.

Ultrasound and the EHR:
Ultrasound images can be integrated into EHR systems, allowing healthcare providers to:

- **Review ultrasound images alongside other patient data** for a more comprehensive picture of a patient's condition.
- **Track changes in ultrasound images** over time to monitor treatment progress or disease progression.
- **Share ultrasound images electronically** with specialists for consultation, improving care coordination.

The Future of Ultrasound:

Advancements in ultrasound technology are focused on:

- **Improved Image Quality:** New technologies are continually enhancing the resolution and detail of ultrasound images.
- **3D Ultrasound:** 3D ultrasound techniques are providing a more comprehensive view of internal structures.
- **Contrast-Enhanced Ultrasound:** The use of contrast agents can improve visualization of blood flow and certain tissues.

The Big Data Challenge of Medical Images:

Each medical image can be incredibly complex, containing vast amounts of data points representing different tissue densities, textures, and functionalities. As the resolution and sophistication of imaging techniques increase, so does the data volume. This presents a significant challenge:

- **Storage Requirements:** Storing this ever-growing data requires robust and scalable storage solutions. Traditional methods like physical storage media are becoming increasingly inadequate.

- **Data Management:** Efficiently managing, organizing, and retrieving medical images is crucial for clinical workflows. Healthcare institutions need robust data management systems to ensure easy access for authorized personnel.
- **Network Bandwidth:** Sharing and transferring large medical image files across networks can be time-consuming and resource-intensive. Efficient data transfer protocols and high-bandwidth networks are essential.

Unlocking the Potential: Solutions for Medical Image Storage and Analysis

Here's how healthcare is tackling the medical imaging data challenge:

- **Cloud Storage:** Cloud computing offers a scalable and cost-effective solution for storing vast amounts of medical imaging data. Cloud platforms provide secure, readily accessible storage with minimal on-site infrastructure requirements.
- **Data Compression Techniques:** Utilizing advanced data compression algorithms can significantly reduce the file size of medical images without compromising diagnostic quality. This optimizes storage requirements and facilitates faster data transfer.
- **Image Archiving and Communication Systems (PACS):** PACS are specialized systems designed for storing, managing, retrieving, and sharing medical images within healthcare institutions. PACS streamline workflows, improve accessibility, and ensure the integrity of medical images.

- **Artificial Intelligence (AI):** AI, particularly deep learning, is revolutionizing medical image analysis. AI algorithms can analyze large datasets of medical images to identify subtle patterns and abnormalities that might be missed by the human eye. This can lead to earlier and more accurate diagnoses.

The Future of Medical Imaging: A Symphony of Technology and Expertise

The future of medical imaging is bright, with advancements in technology and data management fostering a more efficient and effective diagnostic environment:

- **Advanced Imaging Techniques:** New imaging modalities with even higher resolution and functional capabilities are constantly under development, promising even deeper insights into the human body.
- **AI-powered Diagnostics:** As AI algorithms become more sophisticated, they will play an increasingly prominent role in medical image analysis, assisting radiologists in diagnosis and potentially leading to personalized treatment recommendations.
- **Improved Data Interoperability:** Standardized data formats and interoperable systems will facilitate seamless sharing of medical images across healthcare institutions, improving collaboration and patient care coordination.

By harnessing the power of technology and innovative solutions for storage and analysis, medical imaging is poised to continue its transformative journey, shaping the future of diagnostics and propelling healthcare towards a new era of precision medicine.

Wearable Devices and Remote Monitoring: The rise of wearable devices and remote monitoring technologies is generating a continuous stream of patient data, including heart rate, blood pressure, and activity levels.

The healthcare landscape is witnessing a surge in the use of wearable devices and remote monitoring technologies. These advancements are fundamentally changing the way patient health data is collected, analyzed, and utilized. Unlike traditional methods relying on periodic check-ups, wearables and remote monitoring create a continuous stream of real-world health data, offering a more comprehensive picture of an individual's health.

A Fountain of Physiological Information:

Wearable devices come in various forms, from fitness trackers and smartwatches to smart clothing and medical-grade sensors. These devices can monitor a wide range of physiological parameters, including:

- **Vital Signs:** Heart rate, blood pressure, oxygen saturation, and respiratory rate.
- **Activity Levels:** Steps taken, distance covered, calories burned, and sleep patterns.
- **Electrocardiogram (ECG):** Monitors electrical activity of the heart, aiding in arrhythmia detection.
- **Blood Glucose Levels:** Continuous monitoring for diabetic patients.
- **Electroencephalogram (EEG):** Measures brain activity, used for sleep monitoring and epilepsy management.

Remote Monitoring Platforms: Expanding the Reach of Care

Remote monitoring platforms act as the nerve center for wearable device data. This data is wirelessly transmitted to these platforms, where it can be:

- **Visualized:** Data is presented in user-friendly formats like graphs and charts, allowing patients and healthcare providers to easily track health trends.
- **Analyzed:** Advanced algorithms can identify patterns and potential health concerns, prompting further investigation or intervention.
- **Actionable Insights:** Remote monitoring platforms can generate alerts or notifications for healthcare providers or patients in case of concerning readings or trends.

The Advantages of Continuous Health Monitoring:

This continuous stream of real-time data offers a multitude of benefits for both patients and healthcare providers:

- **Improved Disease Management:** For chronic conditions like diabetes, heart disease, and asthma, continuous monitoring allows for proactive management and timely adjustments to medication or treatment plans.
- **Early Detection of Health Issues:** Wearables can pick up subtle changes in vital signs or activity levels that might indicate potential health issues, enabling earlier intervention and improved outcomes.
- **Personalized Care:** The wealth of data collected can be used to personalize healthcare plans by tailoring them to an individual's unique health profile and lifestyle.
- **Empowered Patients:** Access to their own health data empowers patients to take a more active role in their

health management and decision-making.

- **Reduced Healthcare Costs:** Early detection and prevention of health complications can potentially lead to reduced healthcare costs in the long run.

Challenges and Considerations:

While promising, wearable devices and remote monitoring technologies present certain challenges:

- **Data Security and Privacy:** Ensuring the security and privacy of sensitive patient health data is paramount. Robust cybersecurity measures and clear data governance practices are crucial.
- **Data Overload and Alert Fatigue:** The constant stream of data can be overwhelming for both patients and healthcare providers. Effective data filtering and prioritization strategies are necessary.
- **Accuracy and Reliability:** The accuracy and reliability of wearable device data can vary depending on the device and user factors. Calibration and validation are essential.
- **Accessibility and Equity:** Cost and technological literacy can be barriers to access for certain populations. Equitable access to these technologies is important.

The Future of Wearable Devices and Remote Monitoring:

The future of wearable devices and remote monitoring is brimming with potential:

- **Integration with AI:** Artificial intelligence can be used to analyze vast amounts of data from wearables, identifying trends and predicting potential health risks with even greater accuracy.

- **Advanced Sensors and Devices:** The development of more sophisticated sensors and devices will lead to even more comprehensive health monitoring capabilities.
- **Remote Patient Engagement:** Wearables and remote monitoring can be leveraged to create remote patient engagement programs, promoting self-care and preventive health practices.

As wearable devices and remote monitoring technologies continue to evolve and challenges are addressed, they hold the promise of revolutionizing healthcare delivery, fostering a future of proactive, data-driven care that empowers patients and healthcare providers alike.

Genomics: The field of genomics is rapidly expanding, leading to the generation of massive datasets containing individuals' genetic information.

This data deluge presents both challenges and opportunities for the healthcare industry.

Challenges:

- **Data Storage and Management:** Storing and managing the ever-growing volume of data requires significant investment in infrastructure and IT expertise.
- **Data Integration and Standardization:** Healthcare data comes from a variety of sources and often exists in different formats. Integrating and standardizing this data is crucial for effective analysis.
- **Data Security and Privacy:** Protecting sensitive patient data from cyberattacks and breaches is a paramount concern in the age of big data.

- **Data Analytics Expertise:** Extracting meaningful insights from the vast amount of healthcare data requires skilled data analysts and data scientists.

Opportunities:

- **Improved Diagnosis and Treatment:** By analyzing large datasets, deep learning algorithms can identify patterns and trends that might not be apparent to human doctors. This can lead to earlier and more accurate diagnoses, as well as the development of personalized treatment plans.
- **Predictive Analytics:** Healthcare data can be used to predict future health risks for individuals and populations. This allows for early intervention and preventive measures to be taken.
- **Enhanced Research and Development:** Deep learning can analyze vast datasets of medical research to accelerate drug discovery and development of new treatments.
- **Improved Patient Engagement:** Data from wearable devices and patient portals can be used to empower patients to take a more active role in managing their health.

Despite the challenges, the potential benefits of harnessing the data deluge in healthcare are vast. By developing innovative solutions for data management, analytics, and security, the healthcare industry can unlock the power of this data to improve patient care and transform healthcare delivery.

CHAPTER FOUR

RISE OF DEEP LEARNING

Deep learning, a subfield of artificial intelligence (AI), has emerged as a powerful tool for unlocking the potential of big data in various industries, and healthcare is no exception. Here's a closer look at the rise of deep learning and its growing significance in the medical field:

From Artificial Neural Networks to Deep Learning:

The foundation of deep learning lies in artificial neural networks (ANNs), which are loosely inspired by the structure and function of the human brain. These networks consist of interconnected nodes (artificial neurons) that process information in layers. However, traditional ANNs with few layers struggled to handle complex tasks.

The breakthrough came with the development of deep learning architectures. These models employ a significantly higher number of layers, allowing them to learn intricate patterns and relationships within vast amounts of data. This multi-layered approach enables deep learning to excel in tasks like image recognition, natural language processing, and – crucially for healthcare – medical data analysis.

Factors Fueling Deep Learning's Rise in Healthcare:

Several factors have contributed to the rapid adoption of deep learning in healthcare:

Increased Computing Power: The ever-increasing computing power of modern computers is a game-changer for artificial intelligence, particularly in the realm of deep learning. Here's how this enhanced processing muscle is revolutionizing AI:

The Bottleneck of Deep Learning:

Deep learning algorithms are inspired by the structure and function of the human brain. They consist of artificial neural networks with multiple layers, and require massive amounts of data to train effectively. In the past, processing these vast datasets for complex deep learning models was a significant bottleneck.

The Rise of Powerful Processors:

The exponential growth in computing power, driven by advancements in chip manufacturing and processor architecture, has alleviated this bottleneck. Modern computers with powerful CPUs, GPUs (Graphics Processing Units), and specialized AI accelerators can process information significantly faster than ever before.

How Increased Processing Power Benefits Deep Learning:

- **Faster Training:** With more powerful processors, deep learning algorithms can train on massive datasets in a fraction of the time previously required. This allows for more complex models to be developed and iterated upon quickly.

- **Handling Larger Datasets:** The ability to process information faster opens the door to utilizing even larger and more diverse datasets for training deep learning models. This can lead to more robust and generalizable models that perform better on unseen data.

- **Deeper and More Complex Models:** As processing limitations recede, researchers can design deeper neural networks with more layers. These complex models can potentially capture more intricate patterns within the data, leading to superior performance on tasks like image recognition, natural language processing, and even protein folding for drug discovery.

Real-World Applications:

The impact of increased computing power on deep learning is evident across various industries:

- **Medical Diagnosis:** Deep learning algorithms are being trained on vast medical image datasets (X-rays, MRIs) to assist healthcare professionals in earlier and more accurate diagnoses.
- **Personalized Medicine:** Deep learning can analyze a patient's medical history, genetic data, and lifestyle factors to predict disease risk and tailor treatment plans.
- **Drug Discovery:** By analyzing complex biological data, deep learning can accelerate drug discovery and development processes.
- **Autonomous Vehicles:** Deep learning is crucial for training the complex algorithms that enable self-driving cars to navigate roads and perceive their surroundings.
- **Financial Services:** Deep learning is used for fraud detection, algorithmic trading, and personalized financial recommendations.

Challenges and Considerations:

While increased computing power is a boon for deep learning, challenges remain:

- **Data Security and Privacy:** As AI models are trained on ever-larger datasets, ensuring data security and privacy becomes paramount.
- **Explainability of AI Decisions:** Deep learning models can sometimes be like black boxes, making it difficult to understand how they arrive at specific decisions. This lack of explainability can raise ethical concerns, particularly in high-stakes applications.
- **Accessibility of Computing Resources:** Access to powerful computing resources can be expensive, potentially limiting the development of cutting-edge AI models by smaller companies and research institutions.

The Future of Deep Learning and Computing Power:
The co-evolution of deep learning algorithms and ever-increasing computing power holds immense promise for the future. We can expect advancements in:

- **Neuromorphic Computing:** Hardware specifically designed to mimic the human brain's structure and function could revolutionize deep learning efficiency.
- **Quantum Computing:** While still in its early stages, quantum computing has the potential to tackle problems beyond the reach of classical computers, potentially leading to breakthroughs in AI capabilities.

In conclusion, the ever-growing processing capabilities of modern computers are acting as a jet fuel for deep learning. This powerful combination is transforming various fields and pushing the boundaries of what AI can achieve. As we move forward, addressing ethical considerations and ensuring responsible development will be crucial to harnessing the full potential of deep learning for the benefit of society.

Availability of Medical Data: The vast amount of medical data generated in healthcare today, often referred to as the data deluge, serves as the critical fuel for deep learning algorithms. This data provides the raw material for these algorithms to learn, identify patterns, and ultimately improve their ability to analyze and interpret medical information. Here's a closer look at this symbiotic relationship:

Why Medical Data Matters for Deep Learning:

- **Training Data:** Deep learning algorithms are essentially data-driven. The more high-quality medical data they are trained on, the better they become at recognizing patterns, predicting outcomes, and performing specific tasks.
- **Variety is Key:** A diverse dataset encompassing various patient demographics, medical conditions, and treatment responses is crucial for developing robust deep learning models that can generalize well to unseen data.
- **Real-World Data:** Electronic health records (EHRs), medical imaging data (X-rays, MRIs), and genomic data all contribute to a rich pool of real-world medical data that can be harnessed for deep learning applications.

How Deep Learning Leverages Medical Data:

- **Medical Image Analysis:** Deep learning excels at image recognition and can be trained on vast collections of medical images to automate tasks like tumor detection in X-rays or identifying abnormalities in MRIs. This can assist radiologists in diagnosis and improve accuracy.

- **Drug Discovery:** Deep learning can analyze complex biological data sets and patient information to identify potential drug targets and accelerate the drug discovery process.
- **Personalized Medicine:** By analyzing a patient's medical history, genomics data, and lifestyle factors, deep learning algorithms can aid in predicting disease risk and tailoring treatment plans for individual patients.
- **Epidemic Prediction:** Deep learning models can be trained on historical disease outbreak data to identify patterns and predict potential future outbreaks, allowing for earlier intervention and mitigation strategies.

Challenges of Utilizing Medical Data for Deep Learning:

- **Data Quality and Standardization:** Medical data can be riddled with inconsistencies, errors, and missing information. Ensuring data quality and standardization across different healthcare institutions is crucial for effective deep learning applications.
- **Data Privacy and Security:** As deep learning models handle sensitive patient data, robust privacy and security measures are essential to protect patient information and comply with data privacy regulations.
- **Explainability and Bias:** Deep learning models can sometimes be like "black boxes", making it difficult to understand how they arrive at specific conclusions. This lack of explainability can be a concern, especially in

high-stakes medical applications. Additionally, biases present in the underlying medical data can be perpetuated by deep learning models if not carefully addressed.

The Future of Medical Data and Deep Learning:

As data collection and management practices improve, and ethical considerations are addressed, the synergy between medical data and deep learning holds immense promise for the future of healthcare:

- **Improved Diagnostics:** Deep learning can assist healthcare professionals in earlier and more accurate diagnoses, leading to better patient outcomes.
- **Advanced Treatment Planning:** Deep learning models can analyze complex medical data to personalize treatment plans and predict potential responses to therapy.
- **Drug Development Revolution:** Deep learning can accelerate drug discovery and development by identifying promising drug targets and optimizing clinical trials.
- **Population Health Management:** Deep learning can analyze vast datasets to identify trends and predict disease outbreaks, enabling proactive public health interventions.

By harnessing the power of medical data and deep learning responsibly, we can usher in a new era of personalized, data-driven healthcare with the potential to improve patient outcomes and transform healthcare delivery.

The Potential Impact of Deep Learning on Healthcare:

Deep learning holds immense promise for revolutionizing healthcare in several ways. Here are some key areas of potential impact:

- **Enhanced Medical Imaging Analysis:** Deep learning algorithms can analyze medical images like X-rays, MRIs, and CT scans with unprecedented accuracy, aiding in earlier disease detection and improved diagnosis.
- **Personalized Medicine:** By analyzing a patient's medical history, genetic data, and lifestyle factors, deep learning can help tailor treatment plans to their unique needs.
- **Drug Discovery Acceleration:** Deep learning can analyze vast molecular datasets to identify promising drug candidates, potentially leading to faster and more efficient drug development.
- **Improved Clinical Trials:** Deep learning can be used to select the most suitable patients for clinical trials, leading to more effective and streamlined research.
- **Robotic-Assisted Surgery:** Deep learning algorithms can be utilized to guide robotic surgical instruments with greater precision, potentially improving surgical outcomes.

The Rise Continues:

Deep learning is still a rapidly evolving field. As research continues and algorithms become more sophisticated, we can expect even greater advancements in its applications within healthcare. This technology has the potential to transform how we diagnose diseases, develop treatments, and ultimately deliver patient care.

CHAPTER FIVE

DEEP LEARNING'S IMPACT ON MEDICAL IMAGING

Enhanced Diagnostic Accuracy:

Deep learning is revolutionizing the field of medical imaging by enabling computers to analyze scans and images with remarkable accuracy, often surpassing human capabilities. This translates to significant improvements in diagnosing various diseases, leading to earlier intervention and better patient outcomes. Here are some specific examples:

Cancer Detection:

- **Earlier and More Accurate Identification:** Deep learning algorithms can analyze mammograms, lung scans, and other images to detect subtle abnormalities associated with cancer. This allows for earlier detection of the disease when it's most treatable.
- **Reduced False Positives and Negatives:** Deep learning can improve the specificity of cancer screenings, reducing the number of false positives that lead to

unnecessary biopsies and anxiety for patients. Additionally, it can help identify cancers that might be missed by human radiologists.

- **Improved Risk Stratification**: By analyzing tumor characteristics alongside other patient data, deep learning can help predict the aggressiveness of a cancer. This information can be crucial for guiding treatment decisions.

Neurological Diagnosis:

- **Early Detection of Neurodegenerative Diseases:** Deep learning algorithms can analyze brain scans to identify early signs of Alzheimer's disease, Parkinson's disease, and other neurodegenerative conditions. This allows for earlier intervention and potentially slows disease progression.
- **Improved Stroke Diagnosis:** Deep learning can analyze brain scans to differentiate between different types of strokes, such as ischemic and hemorrhagic stroke. This information is critical for determining the most appropriate treatment course.
- **Automating Lesion Detection:** Deep learning algorithms can automate the detection of lesions in brain scans, freeing up radiologists' time to focus on more complex tasks and patient care.

Beyond Cancer and Neurology:
The potential of deep learning extends to other areas of diagnostic imaging as well. For instance, deep learning algorithms are being developed to analyze retinal scans for diabetic retinopathy, a leading cause of blindness, and chest X-rays for pneumonia and other lung diseases.

Challenges and Considerations:

While deep learning offers tremendous promise for improving diagnostic accuracy, some challenges need to be addressed:

- **Data Bias:** Deep learning algorithms are only as good as the data they are trained on. Biased datasets can lead to biased algorithms that perpetuate existing disparities in healthcare.
- **Explainability and Transparency:** Deep learning models can be complex and difficult to interpret. It's crucial to develop methods for explaining how these models arrive at their conclusions to ensure trust in their diagnostic capabilities.
- **Regulatory Landscape:** As deep learning plays an increasingly prominent role in medical diagnosis, clear regulatory frameworks need to be established to ensure the safety and efficacy of these technologies.

Personalized Treatment Planning:

Traditionally, treatment plans have often been a "one-size-fits-all" approach based on the average response of a patient population to a specific condition. However, with the rise of deep learning, healthcare is moving towards a more personalized approach to treatment planning. This section explores how deep learning empowers the creation of customized treatment plans for individual patients.

Harnessing the Power of Data:

Deep learning algorithms can analyze vast amounts of patient data, including:

- **Medical history:** Past diagnoses, medications, and treatment responses.

- **Genetic data:** Identifying potential genetic markers that influence response to specific treatments.
- **Lifestyle factors:** Diet, exercise habits, and environmental exposures.
- **Imaging data:** Analyzing medical scans to understand the disease's characteristics.

By integrating and analyzing this diverse data, deep learning models can identify complex patterns and relationships that might not be evident to human doctors. This allows for a more comprehensive understanding of each patient's unique condition and how they might respond to different treatment options.

Benefits of Personalized Treatment Planning:

- **Improved Efficacy:** By tailoring treatment plans to each patient's specific needs, deep learning can potentially increase the effectiveness of treatment. This can lead to better patient outcomes and a higher chance of achieving remission.
- **Reduced Side Effects:** Personalized treatment plans can minimize the risk of unnecessary or ineffective treatments, reducing the burden of side effects on patients.
- **Optimizing Resource Allocation:** Deep learning can help identify patients who are more likely to benefit from specific therapies, allowing for a more efficient allocation of healthcare resources.
- **Empowering Patients:** Personalized treatment plans allow for a more collaborative approach to care, where patients are actively involved in decision-making based on their individual circumstances.

Examples of Deep Learning in Personalized Medicine:

- **Cancer Treatment:** Deep learning can analyze a patient's tumor characteristics and genetic profile to predict their response to chemotherapy, radiation therapy, or targeted therapies.
- **Cardiovascular Disease:** By analyzing patient data, deep learning can help determine the most appropriate treatment approach for heart disease, such as medication, lifestyle modifications, or surgical intervention.
- **Mental Health:** Deep learning can be used to personalize treatment plans for mental health conditions like depression and anxiety, taking into account individual factors and tailoring therapy approaches.

Challenges and Considerations:

- **Data Privacy and Security:** Ensuring patient data privacy and security is paramount when using deep learning for personalized medicine.
- **Explainability and Trust:** It's crucial for doctors to understand the rationale behind deep learning recommendations to maintain trust in their use for treatment planning.
- **Addressing Algorithmic Bias:** Deep learning algorithms trained on biased datasets can perpetuate existing healthcare disparities. Mitigating bias in data and algorithms is essential for ensuring equitable access to personalized medicine.

The Future of Personalized Treatment Planning:

Deep learning is still evolving, but the potential for personalized treatment planning is vast. As research continues and algorithms become more sophisticated, we can expect even greater advancements in tailoring treatment plans to each patient's unique needs. This approach holds immense promise for improving patient outcomes, reducing healthcare costs, and ushering in a new era of precision medicine.

CHAPTER SIX

BEYOND IMAGES: DEEP LEARNING'S DIVERSE APPLICATIONS

Drug Discovery Acceleration:

Drug discovery is a notoriously slow and expensive process. Traditionally, it can take over a decade and billions of dollars to bring a new drug to market. This lengthy timeline translates to delays in treating patients and missed opportunities to address critical medical needs. However, deep learning is emerging as a game-changer in drug discovery, offering significant potential to accelerate the process.

The Bottlenecks in Drug Discovery:

Here are some key challenges that have plagued drug discovery for decades:

- **Target Identification:** Identifying the right biological target for a drug is crucial, but it can be a complex and time-consuming process.

- **Lead Generation and Optimization:** Finding promising drug candidates (leads) and optimizing them for efficacy and safety is another major hurdle.
- **Clinical Trials:** Clinical trials are expensive and can fail at various stages, further extending the drug development timeline.

Deep Learning to the Rescue:

Deep learning offers several tools to address these bottlenecks and accelerate drug discovery:

- **Target Identification:** Deep learning algorithms can analyze vast datasets of biological information to identify potential drug targets associated with specific diseases. This can save valuable time and resources compared to traditional methods.
- **Virtual Screening:** Deep learning can be used for virtual screening of large libraries of chemical compounds, identifying those with the potential to interact with the target molecule and produce a therapeutic effect. This significantly reduces the need for expensive and time-consuming laboratory experiments.
- **Predictive Modeling:** Deep learning models can predict the properties of potential drug candidates, such as their efficacy, toxicity, and side effects. This allows researchers to prioritize the most promising candidates for further development.
- **Repurposing Existing Drugs:** Deep learning can help identify new uses for existing drugs, potentially leading to faster development and approval times.

Benefits of Deep Learning-Driven Drug Discovery:

- **Faster Development Timelines:** By streamlining various stages of the process, deep learning can significantly reduce the time it takes to bring a new drug to market. This can expedite patient access to potentially life-saving treatments.
- **Reduced Costs:** Deep learning can help eliminate the need for many traditional laboratory experiments, potentially leading to significant cost savings in drug development.
- **Improved Success Rates:** Deep learning can help identify more promising drug candidates with higher chances of success in clinical trials.

Examples of Deep Learning in Drug Discovery:

- **Freenome:** This company uses deep learning to analyze blood tests and identify early signs of cancer, allowing for earlier intervention and potentially leading to the development of new cancer therapies.
- **Insilico Medicine:** This company utilizes deep learning for virtual screening of drug candidates, aiming to accelerate the discovery of new medications for various diseases.
- **BenevolentAI:** This company leverages deep learning to analyze vast datasets of scientific literature and identify novel drug targets and treatment approaches.

Challenges and Considerations:

- **Data Quality and Quantity:** Deep learning algorithms are reliant on high-quality and comprehensive data sets for training. Ensuring the accuracy and completeness of data is crucial for reliable results.

- **Interpretability of Deep Learning Models:** Understanding the reasoning behind deep learning predictions is important for scientists to make informed decisions about drug candidates.
- **Regulatory Landscape:** As deep learning plays an increasingly prominent role in drug discovery, clear regulatory frameworks need to be established to ensure the safety and efficacy of new drugs developed using this technology.

The Future of Drug Discovery:

Deep learning holds immense promise for revolutionizing drug discovery. By accelerating the process, reducing costs, and improving success rates, this technology can lead to the development of new life-saving treatments for patients in need. As research continues and deep learning algorithms become more sophisticated, we can expect even greater advancements in this crucial field.

Electronic Health Records Analysis (EHRs):

Electronic health records (EHRs) have become the backbone of modern healthcare. They contain a wealth of information about a patient's medical history, including diagnoses, medications, lab results, allergies, and immunization records. However, this data often remains locked away in its raw form, untapped for its full potential. Deep learning can unlock the hidden gems within EHR data, offering valuable insights to improve patient care and healthcare delivery.

Unlocking the Potential of EHRs:

Deep learning excels at analyzing complex and unstructured data, making it a perfect tool for extracting meaningful insights from EHRs. Here are some ways deep learning can be applied to EHR data:

- **Risk Stratification:** Deep learning algorithms can analyze a patient's EHR data to identify those at high risk for developing certain diseases, such as heart disease, diabetes, or chronic kidney disease. This allows for early intervention and preventive measures to be taken.
- **Readmission Prediction:** By analyzing past admissions and other patient data, deep learning can predict which patients are more likely to be readmitted to the hospital. This allows for targeted interventions to reduce readmission rates and improve patient outcomes.
- **Medication Adherence Monitoring:** Deep learning can analyze medication refill data in EHRs to identify patients who might not be adhering to their prescribed medications. This allows healthcare providers to intervene and address the reasons for non-adherence.
- **Personalized Treatment Planning:** Deep learning can analyze a patient's EHR data alongside other sources, like genomic data, to personalize treatment plans based on their individual characteristics and medical history.

Benefits of Deep Learning-Driven EHR Analysis:

- **Improved Patient Care:** Early identification of potential health risks and medication adherence issues allows for proactive measures, leading to better patient outcomes.
- **Enhanced Clinical Decision-Making:** Deep learning insights can empower healthcare providers to make more informed decisions about patient care.
- **Reduced Healthcare Costs:** By identifying high-risk patients and promoting medication adherence, deep learning can help reduce hospital readmission rates and associated healthcare costs.

- **Population Health Management:** Deep learning can analyze large datasets of EHRs to identify trends and patterns across populations. This information can be used to develop targeted public health initiatives.

Challenges and Considerations:

- **Data Quality and Standardization:** The quality and standardization of data within EHRs can vary significantly. This inconsistency can impact the accuracy of deep learning models.
- **Data Privacy and Security:** EHR data is highly sensitive, and robust safeguards are needed to ensure patient privacy and data security when using it for deep learning analysis.
- **Explainability and Transparency:** Understanding the rationale behind deep learning predictions derived from EHR data is crucial for building trust in this technology.

The Future of EHR Analysis:

Deep learning is transforming how we utilize EHR data. By unlocking the vast potential of this information, we can move towards a future of more proactive, personalized, and data-driven healthcare. As data quality improves, regulations evolve, and deep learning algorithms become more sophisticated, EHR analysis has the potential to revolutionize healthcare delivery for both patients and providers.

Unlocking the Potential of Genomics:

Genomics, the study of an organism's complete set of genetic instructions, has revolutionized our understanding of health and disease. By analyzing an individual's genetic makeup, we can gain insights into their predisposition to certain diseases, potential drug responses, and even personalized treatment plans. However, analyzing vast amounts of genomic data can be a complex and time-consuming task. This is where deep learning steps in, acting as the key to unlocking the full potential of genomics in healthcare.

Deep Learning Meets Genomics:

Deep learning algorithms excel at identifying patterns and relationships within large datasets. When applied to genomics, this translates to several exciting possibilities:

- **Disease Risk Prediction:** Deep learning can analyze an individual's genome to identify genetic variations associated with an increased risk of developing specific diseases like cancer, Alzheimer's, or heart disease. This allows for early intervention and preventive measures.
- **Drug Response Prediction:** Deep learning can analyze a patient's genetic profile alongside information about their disease to predict their potential response to various medications. This can help healthcare providers choose the most effective treatments and avoid those with a higher risk of side effects.
- **Personalized Medicine:** By combining genomic data with other patient information, deep learning can contribute to creating personalized treatment plans tailored to an individual's unique genetic makeup.
- **Drug Discovery:** Deep learning can analyze vast genomic datasets to identify potential drug targets and accelerate the development of new therapies.

Benefits of Deep Learning-Driven Genomics Analysis:

- **Proactive Healthcare:** Predicting disease risks allows for early intervention and potentially prevents the onset of illness.
- **Improved Treatment Selection:** Identifying the most effective medications for each patient can significantly improve treatment outcomes and reduce side effects.
- **Advancements in Personalized Medicine:** Deep learning unlocks the potential for truly personalized treatment plans, catering to each patient's unique genetic makeup.
- **Faster Drug Development:** Deep learning can streamline drug discovery by identifying promising drug targets based on genomic insights.

Challenges and Considerations:

- **Data Privacy and Security:** Genomic data is highly sensitive and requires robust security measures to protect patient privacy.
- **Data Interpretation:** Deep learning models can be complex, and interpreting their predictions in the context of genomics requires expertise in both fields.
- **Addressing Algorithmic Bias:** Biases in training data can lead to biased predictions. Mitigating bias is crucial for ensuring equitable access to the benefits of deep learning-driven genomics analysis.
- **Regulatory Landscape:** As deep learning plays an increasingly important role in genomic analysis, clear regulations need to be established to ensure the responsible and ethical use of this technology.

The Future of Deep Learning and Genomics:

The convergence of deep learning and genomics holds immense promise for revolutionizing healthcare. As research progresses and deep learning algorithms become more sophisticated, we can expect even greater advancements in disease prediction, personalized medicine, and drug discovery. This powerful combination has the potential to unlock a new era of preventive, precise, and individualized healthcare for all.

Virtual Assistants and Chatbots for Improved Patient Engagement: Empowering Patients in the Digital Age

The healthcare landscape is undergoing a digital transformation, and patients are increasingly seeking information and managing their health online. Virtual assistants (VAs) and chatbots powered by deep learning are emerging as valuable tools for improving patient engagement and communication.

What are Virtual Assistants and Chatbots?

- **Virtual Assistants (VAs):** VAs are AI-powered software applications that can simulate conversation with users through voice or text commands. They can be accessed through smartphones, smart speakers, or dedicated devices and can perform various tasks like scheduling appointments, refilling prescriptions, or answering basic health questions.
- **Chatbots:** Chatbots are conversational interfaces that simulate interaction with a human agent through text-based messaging platforms. They can be integrated into healthcare provider websites, mobile apps, or messaging services to provide patients with information, answer frequently asked questions, and offer basic support.

How Deep Learning Empowers VAs and Chatbots:

Deep learning algorithms enable VAs and chatbots to:

- **Understand Natural Language:** Deep learning allows VAs and chatbots to process and respond to natural language queries, making interactions more user-friendly and intuitive for patients.
- **Personalize Communication:** By analyzing user data and past interactions, deep learning can personalize the experience, tailoring responses and recommendations to each patient's specific needs.
- **Learn and Improve Over Time:** Deep learning models can continuously learn and improve their responses based on user interactions and feedback, leading to more accurate and helpful interactions over time.

Benefits of VAs and Chatbots in Healthcare:

- **Improved Patient Engagement:** VAs and chatbots can provide 24/7 access to information and support, empowering patients to take a more active role in managing their health.
- **Enhanced Convenience:** Scheduling appointments, refilling prescriptions, or getting answers to basic questions can be done efficiently through VAs and chatbots, saving patients time and effort.
- **Reduced Burden on Healthcare Staff:** Automating routine tasks like appointment scheduling frees up healthcare professionals' time to focus on more complex patient care needs.
- **Streamlined Communication:** VAs and chatbots can be used for appointment reminders, medication adherence support, and post-discharge follow-up, improving communication between patients and healthcare

providers.

Examples of VAs and Chatbots in Action:

- **Scheduling appointments:** A patient can use a VA to schedule an appointment by simply saying "schedule a physical for next week."
- **Refilling prescriptions:** A chatbot can be used to refill prescriptions by prompting the patient for their medication information and securely submitting the request.
- **Providing health information:** A VA can answer basic health questions about symptoms, medications, or healthy living practices.
- **Mental health support:** Chatbots can offer mental health support by providing resources, self-help tools, and directing users to appropriate services.

Challenges and Considerations:

- **Data Privacy and Security:** Protecting sensitive patient information is paramount when using VAs and chatbots. Robust security measures are essential to maintain trust.
- **Technical Limitations:** While natural language processing has improved, VAs and chatbots may still struggle with complex questions or nuanced language.
- **Limited Emotional Intelligence:** VAs and chatbots cannot replace human interaction for complex emotional situations or providing empathy and support.

The Future of VAs and Chatbots in Healthcare:

VAs and chatbots are not meant to replace human healthcare professionals, but rather to act as valuable assistants, empowering patients and improving communication. As deep learning technologies continue to evolve, we can expect VAs and chatbots to become even more sophisticated, offering a wider range of services and functionalities to enhance patient engagement and improve overall healthcare delivery.

CHAPTER SEVEN

CHALLENGES AND CONSIDERATIONS

Data Quality and Bias:

Deep learning holds immense promise for revolutionizing healthcare. However, its effectiveness hinges on one crucial factor: data. While the potential of deep learning is vast, the quality and potential biases within the data used to train these algorithms can significantly impact their performance and real-world applications. Here's a closer look at this critical challenge.

The Importance of Data Quality:

Deep learning algorithms are essentially pattern-recognition machines. The quality of the data they are trained on determines the quality of the patterns they learn. Here's how data quality impacts deep learning in healthcare:

Accuracy of Results: Poor quality data, such as missing entries, inconsistencies, or errors, can lead to inaccurate deep learning predictions. This can have serious consequences in healthcare, where even minor errors can impact patient diagnosis and treatment.The accuracy of deep learning predictions in healthcare hinges critically on the quality of the data used to train and run the models.

Poor quality data, riddled with missing entries, inconsistencies, and errors, can lead to inaccurate predictions with potentially serious consequences for patient diagnosis and treatment. Here's a deeper dive into this challenge and potential solutions:

How Poor Data Quality Affects Deep Learning in Healthcare:

- **Garbage In, Garbage Out:** Deep learning models are essentially sophisticated pattern recognition machines. If the data they are trained on is flawed, the patterns they learn will be inaccurate, leading to unreliable predictions.
- **Missing Entries:** Incomplete data can hinder a deep learning model's ability to identify crucial relationships and patterns within the data.
- **Inconsistencies:** Variations in how data is collected, coded, or stored across different healthcare institutions can create inconsistencies that confuse deep learning models.
- **Errors:** Accidental errors or typos in medical data can further skew the results of deep learning analysis.

Consequences of Inaccurate Deep Learning Predictions in Healthcare:

- **Misdiagnosis:** Inaccurate predictions from deep learning models used for image analysis or diagnosis support could lead to misdiagnosis of diseases, potentially delaying or missing critical treatment opportunities.
- **Ineffective Treatment Recommendations:** Deep learning models used for treatment planning or drug

discovery could suggest ineffective or even harmful therapies if the underlying data is flawed.

- **Wasted Resources:** Inaccurate predictions can lead to unnecessary tests, procedures, or medications, wasting valuable healthcare resources.

Strategies for Mitigating the Impact of Poor Data Quality:

- **Data Cleaning and Preprocessing:** Implementing robust data cleaning techniques to identify and rectify errors, inconsistencies, and missing entries in medical data is crucial.
- **Data Standardization:** Establishing standardized data collection, coding, and storage practices across healthcare institutions ensures consistency and improves the quality of data used for deep learning models.
- **Data Validation:** Regularly validating the accuracy and completeness of medical data helps maintain data integrity and prevent errors from creeping into deep learning models.
- **Human-in-the-Loop Approach:** A human-in-the-loop approach, where healthcare professionals review and interpret the recommendations of deep learning models, can help mitigate the impact of potential errors and ensure patient safety.

The Future of Data Quality for Deep Learning in Healthcare:

- **Focus on Data Governance:** Implementing robust data governance frameworks will ensure responsible data collection, storage, and use for deep learning applications in healthcare.

- **Advanced Data Cleaning Techniques:** Advancements in data cleaning techniques, potentially using machine learning itself, can automate error detection and correction, improving data quality.
- **Blockchain Technology:** Blockchain technology has the potential to improve data security, privacy, and traceability, fostering trust in the data used for deep learning models.

Generalizability: Deep learning models trained on limited or biased datasets may not generalize well to real-world scenarios with more diverse patient populations. This can lead to unreliable results and perpetuate existing healthcare disparities.Generalizability is a critical challenge for deep learning models in healthcare. Here's a deeper dive into why generalizability matters and how to address it:

The Importance of Generalizability in Healthcare:

- **Real-World Applicability:** Deep learning models in healthcare need to function effectively in real-world settings with diverse patient populations. If a model is only accurate for the specific data it was trained on, its usefulness is limited.
- **Mitigating Bias:** Biases present in the underlying medical data can be perpetuated by deep learning models if generalizability isn't addressed. This can exacerbate existing healthcare disparities and lead to unfair or inaccurate results for certain patient groups.
- **Responsible Use:** Ensuring generalizability is crucial for the responsible use of deep learning in healthcare,

promoting trust and ethical implementation.

How Limited or Biased Data Hinders Generalizability:

- **Limited Datasets:** Deep learning models trained on datasets that don't encompass the full spectrum of a disease or patient population may struggle to perform well on unseen data, leading to unreliable results.
- **Data Biases:** If the training data disproportionately represents a certain demographic group, the deep learning model may inherit those biases and deliver inaccurate predictions for other populations.

Strategies to Improve Generalizability of Deep Learning Models:

- **Data Augmentation:** Techniques like data augmentation can be used to artificially expand the training dataset by creating variations of existing data points. This helps the model learn from a broader range of scenarios.
- **Multimodal Data Integration:** Training deep learning models on a combination of different data types, such as medical images, electronic health records, and genetic data, can improve generalizability by providing a more comprehensive picture of a patient's condition.
- **External Validation:** Regularly testing and validating deep learning models on external datasets that are more representative of real-world patient populations helps identify and address generalizability issues.
- **Focus on Diverse Datasets:** Actively collecting and utilizing medical data from diverse patient populations is crucial for developing generalizable deep learning models that benefit everyone.

The Future of Generalizability in Deep Learning Healthcare:

- **Standardized Data Collection:** Standardized data collection practices across healthcare institutions can help ensure that deep learning models have access to more representative and generalizable datasets.
- **Focus on Fairness and Explainability:** Incorporating fairness and explainability considerations into the development of deep learning models can help mitigate bias and build trust in their generalizability.
- **Regulatory Oversight:** Regulatory frameworks can play a role in ensuring that deep learning models used in healthcare are developed and deployed with generalizability and fairness in mind.

By acknowledging the generalizability challenge and implementing these strategies, we can work towards developing deep learning models that are truly effective for the entire patient population, promoting a more equitable and evidence-based healthcare system.

Algorithmic Bias: If the training data itself is biased, the deep learning model will inherit those biases. This can lead to unfair or discriminatory outcomes, such as misdiagnoses for certain patient demographics.Algorithmic bias is a critical concern in deep learning for healthcare applications. When the training data itself is biased, the deep learning model essentially learns those biases and replicates them in its predictions. This can have serious consequences, leading to unfair or discriminatory outcomes for certain patient demographics. Let's delve deeper into the issue and explore potential solutions:

Sources of Algorithmic Bias in Healthcare:

- **Historical Biases in Medical Data:** Existing biases in how healthcare is delivered, data is collected, or diagnoses are made can be reflected in medical datasets. For example, if a particular demographic group is underrepresented in a dataset, the model might not perform well for that group.
- **Socioeconomic Factors:** Socioeconomic factors like access to healthcare or insurance can influence the data available for training deep learning models. This can lead to biases that disadvantage certain populations.
- **Algorithmic Design Choices:** The way deep learning models are designed and the features they are trained on can introduce unintended biases. For instance, an algorithm trained on easily identifiable visual features in medical images might miss subtle signs of disease in patients with darker skin tones.

Consequences of Algorithmic Bias in Healthcare:

- **Misdiagnosis and Missed Diagnoses:** If a deep learning model is biased against a certain demographic, it may be more likely to misdiagnose patients from that group or miss their diagnoses altogether.
- **Unequal Treatment Recommendations:** Algorithmic bias can influence treatment recommendations, potentially leading to certain patient groups being denied access to necessary treatments or receiving less effective therapies.
- **Erosion of Trust:** If patients perceive that deep learning models are biased, it can erode trust in healthcare AI and lead to hesitancy in adopting these technologies.

Strategies to Mitigate Algorithmic Bias:

- **Data Cleaning and Balancing:** Techniques like data cleaning to identify and address biases in training data, and data balancing to ensure all demographics are adequately represented, can help mitigate bias.
- **Fairness Metrics and Auditing:** Integrating fairness metrics into the development process and regularly auditing deep learning models for bias can help identify and address potential issues early on.
- **Explainable AI (XAI):** Developing Explainable AI (XAI) techniques that make deep learning models more transparent can help understand how they arrive at decisions and identify potential biases.
- **Human Oversight:** Maintaining a human-in-the-loop approach where healthcare professionals review and interpret the recommendations of deep learning models can help mitigate bias and ensure patient safety.

The Future of Mitigating Algorithmic Bias:

- **Standardized Data Collection:** Standardized data collection practices across healthcare institutions can help reduce the risk of biases creeping into medical datasets used for training deep learning models.
- **Diversity in AI Development Teams:** Encouraging diversity in AI development teams, including data scientists, engineers, and ethicists from various backgrounds, can help identify and address potential biases during model development.
- **Regulatory Frameworks:** Developing robust regulatory frameworks that address algorithmic bias in healthcare AI can promote fairness and responsible development of these technologies.

By acknowledging the dangers of algorithmic bias and implementing these strategies, we can work towards developing deep learning models that are fair, unbiased, and beneficial for all patients. This will ensure that everyone can reap the potential benefits of AI in healthcare and contribute to a more equitable healthcare system.

Examples of Data Quality Issues in Healthcare:

- **Missing or Inaccurate Data:** Patient records may have missing information, typos, or inconsistencies, impacting the accuracy of deep learning analysis.
- **Limited Data Sets:** Studies or datasets used to train deep learning models may not encompass the full spectrum of a disease or patient population.
- **Selection Bias:** The way data is collected can introduce bias. For instance, if a study focuses only on hospitalized patients, it may not represent the broader population with the disease.

Mitigating Data Quality Issues:

- **Data Cleaning and Standardization:** Implementing robust data cleaning and standardization procedures is crucial to ensure data accuracy and consistency.
- **Enhancing Data Collection Practices:** Standardizing data collection protocols and ensuring complete and accurate data entry are essential steps towards improving data quality.
- **Expanding Data Sets:** Efforts should be made to collect more comprehensive and diverse datasets that represent the broader patient population.

The Challenge of Bias:

Bias in healthcare data can arise from various factors, such as:

- **Social Determinants of Health:** Factors like socioeconomic status, race, and ethnicity can influence health outcomes and lead to biased data representations.
- **Historical Biases in Medical Practice:** Existing biases in how diseases are diagnosed or treated can be reflected in healthcare data.
- **Algorithmic Bias:** The algorithms used to collect or analyze data can introduce their own biases.

The Impact of Bias in Deep Learning Healthcare Applications:

- **Misdiagnosis and Missed Cases:** Biased algorithms may lead to misdiagnoses for certain patient demographics, potentially delaying or preventing proper treatment.
- **Unequal Access to Care:** Bias can exacerbate existing disparities in healthcare access, disproportionately impacting vulnerable populations.
- **Erosion of Trust:** If patients perceive bias in deep learning-driven healthcare tools, it can erode trust in these technologies.

Addressing Bias in Deep Learning:

- **Data Auditing and Bias Detection:** Techniques to identify and mitigate bias within datasets are crucial.
- **Algorithmic Fairness:** Developing and employing deep learning algorithms that are less susceptible to bias is an ongoing area of research.

- **Diversity and Inclusion in AI Development:** Including diverse teams in the development and implementation of deep learning healthcare solutions is essential to identify and address potential biases.

Security and Privacy Concerns: Protecting Sensitive Data in Deep Learning Healthcare

Deep learning in healthcare offers immense potential, but it also raises significant concerns regarding security and patient privacy. The vast amount of sensitive medical data involved, coupled with the complexity of deep learning models, necessitates robust safeguards to protect patient information and ensure responsible use of this technology.

Why Security and Privacy Matter:

Healthcare data is highly sensitive, and any breach can have serious consequences for patients. Here's why security and privacy are paramount:

- **Data Breaches:** Cyberattacks targeting healthcare institutions can compromise patient data, leading to identity theft, extortion, or even physical harm.
- **Unauthorized Access:** Deep learning models may be vulnerable to unauthorized access, potentially exposing sensitive patient information.
- **Data Misuse:** There's a risk of patient data being used for unintended purposes, such as targeted advertising or insurance discrimination.

Security Challenges in Deep Learning Healthcare:

- **Data Storage and Transmission:** Ensuring secure storage and transmission of sensitive medical data during collection, analysis, and storage is crucial.

- **Model Security:** Deep learning models themselves can be vulnerable to hacking or manipulation, potentially leading to inaccurate predictions or biased outcomes.
- **Access Control:** Implementing robust access control measures to ensure only authorized personnel can access sensitive patient data is essential.

Privacy Concerns in Deep Learning Healthcare:

- **Patient Consent:** Obtaining clear and informed consent from patients regarding how their data is used for deep learning applications is crucial.
- **Data Anonymization:** Techniques to anonymize patient data while still allowing for meaningful analysis are necessary to protect patient privacy.
- **Transparency and Explainability:** Patients have the right to understand how their data is being used by deep learning models and how it impacts their care.

Mitigating Security and Privacy Risks:

- **Data Encryption:** Encrypting data at rest and in transit can significantly enhance security and reduce the risk of breaches.
- **Regular Security Audits:** Healthcare institutions need to conduct regular security audits to identify and address vulnerabilities in their systems.
- **Strong Authentication:** Implementing multi-factor authentication protocols can prevent unauthorized access to sensitive data.
- **De-identification Techniques:** Techniques like anonymization and pseudonymization can help protect

patient privacy while allowing for data analysis.

- **Regulatory Compliance:** Adherence to relevant data privacy regulations, such as HIPAA, is essential for ensuring responsible data handling.
- **Focus on Transparency:** Healthcare providers and developers of deep learning applications should strive for transparency in data collection and usage practices.

The Future of Security and Privacy in Deep Learning Healthcare:

Security and privacy will remain critical considerations as deep learning continues to evolve in healthcare. By prioritizing robust security measures, implementing strong data governance practices, and fostering transparency, we can build trust in this technology and unlock its full potential to improve patient care while safeguarding sensitive medical information.

Explainability and Transparency in Deep Learning Models: Demystifying the Black Box

Deep learning has emerged as a powerful tool in healthcare, offering advancements in disease diagnosis, drug discovery, and personalized medicine. However, a major hurdle remains: the inherent complexity of deep learning models, often referred to as "black boxes." Explainability and transparency are crucial aspects for ensuring trust and responsible use of this technology in healthcare.

Why Explainability and Transparency Matter:

- **Trust and Acceptance:** If patients and healthcare providers don't understand how deep learning models arrive at their conclusions, they may be hesitant to trust their recommendations.

- **Debugging and Error Correction:** Without understanding the reasoning behind a model's prediction, it's difficult to identify and address potential errors or biases.
- **Regulatory Compliance:** Regulatory bodies may require explainability and transparency to ensure the ethical and responsible use of deep learning in healthcare.

Challenges in Explaining Deep Learning Models:

- **Algorithmic Complexity:** Deep learning models can have intricate layers and connections, making it difficult to understand how they reach a specific output.
- **Data-Driven Nature:** Deep learning models often learn complex patterns from vast amounts of data, making it challenging to pinpoint the exact reason behind a particular prediction.

Approaches to Explainability and Transparency:

- **Feature Importance Analysis:** Identifying which features in the data have the most significant influence on the model's predictions can provide insights into its decision-making process.
- **Attention Mechanisms:** Certain deep learning architectures incorporate attention mechanisms that highlight the specific parts of the input data that the model focuses on for making a prediction.
- **Saliency Maps:** These techniques visually represent which parts of the input data contribute most to the model's output, offering a glimpse into its reasoning process.

- **Counterfactual Explanations:** This approach involves generating hypothetical scenarios where a single aspect of the input is changed, helping to understand how the model's prediction would differ.

Benefits of Explainable Deep Learning in Healthcare:

- **Improved Trust and Adoption:** By understanding how deep learning models work, healthcare providers and patients can feel more confident in their use.
- **Enhanced Clinical Decision-Making:** Explainability can help healthcare professionals understand the rationale behind deep learning recommendations, allowing them to make more informed clinical decisions.
- **Identifying and Mitigating Bias:** Explanation techniques can help identify potential biases within the data or the model itself, enabling corrective measures to be taken.

The Future of Explainable Deep Learning:
Explainability and transparency are ongoing areas of research in deep learning. As these techniques evolve, we can expect to see more interpretable deep learning models that can be readily understood and trusted in healthcare settings. This will pave the way for the wider adoption of deep learning and its responsible integration into various aspects of healthcare delivery.

Additional Considerations:

- **Human-in-the-Loop Approach:** Even with advancements in explainability, it's likely that healthcare will continue to rely on a human-in-the-loop approach, where deep learning models provide insights that are ultimately interpreted and acted upon by medical professionals.

- **The Role of Regulation:** Regulatory bodies may play a role in establishing standards for explainability and transparency in deep learning healthcare applications.

By prioritizing explainability and transparency alongside the development of deep learning models, we can ensure that this powerful technology is used responsibly and ethically to improve patient care and healthcare outcomes.

CHAPTER EIGHT

DEEP LEARNING EMPOWERING R&D

Streamlining the Drug Discovery Pipeline:

The traditional drug discovery pipeline is notoriously slow, expensive, and fraught with failures. It can take over a decade and billions of dollars to bring a new drug to market, creating a significant bottleneck in delivering life-saving treatments to patients. Deep learning is emerging as a game-changer, offering a powerful set of tools to streamline this complex process and accelerate the development of new medications.

Bottlenecks in the Drug Discovery Pipeline:

Here are some key challenges that have plagued drug discovery for decades:

- **Target Identification:** Identifying the right biological target for a drug is crucial, but it can be a complex and time-consuming process.
- **Lead Generation and Optimization:** Finding promising drug candidates (leads) and optimizing them for

efficacy and safety is another major hurdle.

- **Clinical Trials:** Clinical trials are expensive and can fail at various stages, further extending the drug development timeline.

Deep Learning to the Rescue:

Deep learning offers several tools to address these bottlenecks and expedite drug discovery:

- **Target Identification:** Deep learning algorithms can analyze vast datasets of biological information to identify potential drug targets associated with specific diseases. This can save valuable time and resources compared to traditional methods.
- **Virtual Screening:** Deep learning can be used for virtual screening of large libraries of chemical compounds, identifying those with the potential to interact with the target molecule and produce a therapeutic effect. This significantly reduces the need for expensive and time-consuming laboratory experiments.
- **Predictive Modeling:** Deep learning models can predict the properties of potential drug candidates, such as their efficacy, toxicity, and side effects. This allows researchers to prioritize the most promising candidates for further development.
- **Repurposing Existing Drugs:** Deep learning can help identify new uses for existing drugs, potentially leading to faster development and approval times.

Benefits of Deep Learning-Driven Drug Discovery:

- **Faster Development Timelines:** By streamlining various stages of the process, deep learning can significantly reduce the time it takes to bring a new drug to market. This can expedite patient access to potentially life-saving treatments.

- **Reduced Costs:** Deep learning can help eliminate the need for many traditional laboratory experiments, potentially leading to significant cost savings in drug development.
- **Improved Success Rates:** Deep learning can help identify more promising drug candidates with higher chances of success in clinical trials.

Examples of Deep Learning in Drug Discovery:

- **Freenome:** This company uses deep learning to analyze blood tests and identify early signs of cancer, allowing for earlier intervention and potentially leading to the development of new cancer therapies.
- **Insilico Medicine:** This company utilizes deep learning for virtual screening of drug candidates, aiming to accelerate the discovery of new medications for various diseases.
- **BenevolentAI:** This company leverages deep learning to analyze vast datasets of scientific literature and identify novel drug targets and treatment approaches.

Challenges and Considerations:

- **Data Quality and Quantity:** Deep learning algorithms are reliant on high-quality and comprehensive data sets for training. Ensuring the accuracy and completeness of data is crucial for reliable results.
- **Interpretability of Deep Learning Models:** Understanding the reasoning behind deep learning

predictions is important for scientists to make informed decisions about drug candidates.

- **Regulatory Landscape:** As deep learning plays an increasingly prominent role in drug discovery, clear regulatory frameworks need to be established to ensure the safety and efficacy of new drugs developed using this technology.

The Future of Drug Discovery:

Deep learning holds immense promise for revolutionizing drug discovery. By accelerating the process, reducing costs, and improving success rates, this technology can lead to the development of new life-saving treatments for patients in need. As research continues and deep learning algorithms become more sophisticated, we can expect even greater advancements in this crucial field.

Additional Considerations:

- **Collaboration:** Deep learning can foster collaboration between researchers in various disciplines, such as biology, chemistry, and computer science, to accelerate drug discovery efforts.
- **Open-source platforms:** The development of open-source deep learning platforms for drug discovery can facilitate collaboration and accelerate innovation in this field.

By harnessing the power of deep learning alongside other advancements in science and technology, we can move towards a future where new and effective treatments are developed more rapidly, reaching patients who need them most.

Optimizing Clinical Trial Design: Revolutionizing Drug Development with Deep Learning and Innovation

Clinical trials are the cornerstone of evidence-based medicine, ensuring the safety and efficacy of new drugs before they reach patients. However, traditional clinical trial design can be slow, expensive, and prone to inefficiencies. Deep learning and other innovative approaches are emerging to optimize clinical trial design, paving the way for a more streamlined and effective drug development process.

Challenges in Traditional Clinical Trial Design:

- **Patient Recruitment:** Identifying and enrolling a sufficient number of qualified participants can be a major bottleneck, delaying trials and increasing costs.
- **Trial Size and Duration:** Traditional designs often require large patient populations and lengthy trial periods, leading to significant resource investment.
- **Limited Generalizability:** Trials may not adequately represent the real-world patient population, potentially leading to misleading results.

Deep Learning to the Rescue:

Deep learning offers several tools to address these challenges and optimize clinical trial design:

- **Predictive Analytics:** Deep learning models can analyze patient data to predict which individuals are more likely to respond favorably to a new drug, enabling more targeted recruitment and potentially reducing trial size.
- **Real-World Data Integration:** Deep learning can analyze real-world data (RWD) from electronic health records (EHRs) and other sources to identify potential

patients and gain insights into disease progression. This can inform trial design and improve generalizability.

- **Virtual Trial Platforms:** Deep learning can be integrated into virtual trial platforms, allowing for remote patient monitoring and data collection, potentially reducing costs and increasing accessibility for geographically dispersed participants.
- **Adaptive Trial Designs:** Deep learning can be used to develop adaptive trial designs that adjust parameters based on real-time data, potentially leading to more efficient trials and faster drug development.

Other Innovative Approaches:

- **Decentralized Trials:** These trials leverage telemedicine and remote monitoring technologies, allowing patients to participate from their homes or local clinics, potentially increasing accessibility and enrollment rates.
- **Basket Trials:** These trials enroll patients with different genetic mutations or disease subtypes who share a common therapeutic target, allowing for a more efficient evaluation of a drug's effectiveness across diverse patient populations.

Benefits of Optimized Clinical Trial Design:

- **Faster Drug Development:** By streamlining recruitment, reducing trial size, and leveraging RWD, optimized trials can expedite the development of new drugs.
- **Reduced Costs:** More efficient trials can lead to significant cost savings in the drug development process.

- **Improved Trial Success Rates:** Targeted recruitment and better-designed trials can potentially increase the success rate of clinical trials.
- **Enhanced Generalizability:** Integration of RWD and innovative trial designs can lead to results that are more applicable to the real-world patient population.

Examples of Deep Learning and Innovation in Clinical Trials:

- **Syapse:** This company uses deep learning to analyze RWD from EHRs to identify patients who are eligible for clinical trials.
- **Covance:** This company offers decentralized trial solutions that leverage telemedicine and remote monitoring technologies.
- **IQVIA:** This company provides expertise in adaptive trial designs, allowing for adjustments based on real-time data to optimize trial efficiency.

Challenges and Considerations:

- **Data Privacy and Security:** Ensuring patient privacy and data security is paramount when using deep learning and RWD in clinical trials.
- **Regulatory Landscape:** Regulatory frameworks may need to adapt to accommodate innovative trial designs and deep learning applications.
- **Algorithmic Bias:** Deep learning models can inherit biases from the data they are trained on. Mitigating bias is crucial to ensure fair and equitable access to clinical trials.

The Future of Clinical Trial Design:

Deep learning and other innovative approaches hold immense promise for revolutionizing clinical trial design. By optimizing recruitment, leveraging RWD, and adopting more efficient trial structures, we can expedite drug development, reduce costs, and ultimately deliver life-saving treatments to patients faster. As research progresses and regulations evolve, we can expect even greater advancements in this critical area, leading to a future of more efficient, inclusive, and patient-centric clinical trials.

Advancing Personalized Medicine: A Future Tailored to You

Traditionally, medicine has adopted a "one-size-fits-all" approach. However, with the rise of genomics, big data, and deep learning, Personalized Medicine is emerging as a powerful force, promising to revolutionize healthcare by tailoring treatments and prevention strategies to each individual's unique makeup.

Unlocking the Power of You:

Personalized Medicine leverages a multitude of data points to create a holistic picture of an individual's health:

- **Genomics:** Understanding an individual's genetic makeup allows for identifying predispositions to diseases, potential drug responses, and personalized treatment plans.
- **Phenomics:** This includes a patient's medical history, lifestyle factors, and environmental exposures, providing insights into their overall health.
- **Wearable Devices and Biosensors:** These tools can continuously monitor vital signs, activity levels, and other health parameters, offering real-time data for personalized health management.

Benefits of Personalized Medicine:

- **Preventive Healthcare:** Identifying disease risks early allows for preventive measures and interventions, potentially preventing illness altogether.
- **Improved Treatment Selection:** Personalized medicine helps choose the most effective medications and treatment approaches based on an individual's unique genetic profile and response.
- **Reduced Side Effects:** By tailoring treatments, personalized medicine can minimize the risk of adverse reactions and side effects.
- **Empowered Patients:** Personalized medicine fosters a more collaborative approach to healthcare, empowering patients to actively participate in managing their health.

Deep Learning as the Engine:

Deep learning plays a crucial role in analyzing vast amounts of personal health data and unlocking the potential of personalized medicine:

- **Predictive Modeling:** Deep learning can analyze genomic and phenotypic data to predict an individual's risk of developing specific diseases.
- **Drug Response Prediction:** Deep learning can help predict how a patient might respond to different medications, allowing for personalized treatment plans.
- **Tailoring Treatment Doses:** Deep learning algorithms can analyze individual characteristics to determine optimal drug dosages, maximizing efficacy and minimizing side effects.

Examples of Personalized Medicine in Action:

- **Cancer Treatment:** Genetic testing can guide targeted therapies for cancer, attacking the disease at its molecular root.
- **Cardiovascular Disease:** Personalized medicine can identify individuals at high risk of heart disease, allowing for preventive measures and lifestyle adjustments.
- **Mental Health:** Tailoring psychiatric medications based on an individual's genetic profile can lead to more effective treatment and improved outcomes.

Challenges and Considerations:

- **Data Privacy and Security:** Protecting an individual's vast amount of personal health data is paramount. Robust security measures and clear data governance practices are essential.
- **Accessibility and Equity:** Ensuring equitable access to personalized medicine for all populations is crucial to avoid widening healthcare disparities.
- **Evolving Regulatory Landscape:** Regulations need to adapt to accommodate the evolving field of personalized medicine and the use of deep learning for healthcare decision-making.

The Future of Personalized Medicine:

The future of healthcare lies in personalization. As deep learning and data analysis techniques become more sophisticated, and our understanding of the human genome expands, personalized medicine will continue to evolve. Imagine a future where preventive measures are tailored to your unique needs, treatments are optimized for your specific biology, and you are empowered to be an active participant in your own health journey. This is the promise of Personalized Medicine, a future where healthcare becomes truly individualized.

Personalized medicine is a game-changer for the future of healthcare. It's exciting to imagine a world where:

- **Prevention is proactive, not reactive:** Imagine genetic tests identifying your predisposition to certain diseases, allowing doctors to create personalized plans to prevent them entirely.
- **Treatments hit the bullseye:** Drugs and therapies tailored to your specific biology could lead to faster healing, fewer side effects, and overall better outcomes.
- **You're in the driver's seat:** With access to your own health data and digital tools, you can become a more informed and engaged partner in your healthcare decisions.

This personalized approach has the potential to revolutionize how we treat and prevent disease, empowering individuals and improving health outcomes for everyone.

CHAPTER NINE

DEEP LEARNING AND PATIENT ENGAGEMENT

Virtual Assistants and Chatbots: Empowering Patients in the Digital Age

The healthcare landscape is undergoing a digital transformation, and patients are increasingly seeking information and managing their health online. Virtual assistants (VAs) and chatbots powered by deep learning are emerging as valuable tools for improving patient engagement, education, and overall healthcare experience.

How VAs and Chatbots Empower Patients:

- **24/7 Access to Information:** Patients can access basic health information, appointment scheduling tools, and medication reminders anytime, anywhere. This empowers them to take a more proactive role in managing their health.

- **Increased Convenience:** Simple tasks like scheduling appointments, refilling prescriptions, or getting answers to frequently asked questions can be done efficiently through VAs and chatbots, saving patients time and effort.

- **Personalized Support:** Chatbots can offer personalized guidance based on a patient's medical history and current health concerns, directing them to appropriate resources or healthcare professionals.
- **Mental Health Support:** Chatbots can provide basic mental health support by offering self-help tools, connecting users with mental health resources, and reducing the stigma associated with seeking help.
- **Improved Medication Adherence:** VAs can send medication reminders and provide educational content about medications, promoting better adherence and potentially improving treatment outcomes.

Examples of Patient Empowerment through VAs and Chatbots:

- A diabetic patient uses a VA to set reminders for checking blood sugar levels and taking medication.
- A new mother uses a chatbot to get answers to common infant care questions.
- A patient with anxiety uses a mental health chatbot for relaxation techniques and self-management tools.
- An elderly patient uses a VA to schedule a doctor's appointment and get transportation assistance.

Beyond Convenience: The Power of Deep Learning
Deep learning algorithms enable VAs and chatbots to:

- **Understand Natural Language:** They can process and respond to natural language queries, making interactions more user-friendly and intuitive for patients.

- **Provide Personalized Communication**: VAs and chatbots can tailor their responses and recommendations based on a patient's individual needs and medical history.
- **Learn and Improve Over Time**: Deep learning models continuously learn and improve their responses based on user interactions and feedback, leading to more accurate and helpful interactions over time.

Challenges and Considerations:

- **Data Privacy and Security**: Protecting sensitive patient information is paramount. Robust security measures and clear data governance practices are essential.
- **Technical Limitations**: While natural language processing has improved, VAs and chatbots may still struggle with complex inquiries or nuanced language.
- **Limited Emotional Intelligence**: VAs and chatbots cannot replace human interaction for complex emotional situations or providing empathy and support.
- **Digital Divide**: Unequal access to technology and digital literacy can limit the benefits of VAs and chatbots for certain patient populations.

The Future of VAs and Chatbots in Healthcare:

VAs and chatbots are not meant to replace human healthcare professionals, but rather to act as valuable assistants, empowering patients and improving communication. Here's a glimpse into the future:

- **Integration with Wearable Devices**: VAs and chatbots can be integrated with wearable devices to collect real-time health data and provide more personalized recommendations.

- **Advanced AI for Complex Inquiries:** As AI capabilities advance, VAs and chatbots will be able to handle more complex questions and offer more sophisticated support.
- **Multilingual Support:** VAs and chatbots will become more accessible by offering support in multiple languages, catering to diverse patient populations.

By addressing the challenges and harnessing the potential of deep learning, VAs and chatbots can play a transformative role in empowering patients, improving healthcare access, and fostering a more patient-centered healthcare experience.

Wearable Devices and Remote Monitoring:

The rise of wearable devices and advancements in remote monitoring technologies are revolutionizing healthcare delivery. These tools allow healthcare professionals to track patients' health data continuously, even outside the traditional clinical setting. This shift towards remote monitoring offers a multitude of benefits for both patients and providers.

Unlocking the Potential of Wearable Devices:

Wearable devices come in various forms, from fitness trackers to smartwatches and specialized medical devices. They can monitor a wide range of health parameters, including:

- **Heart Rate:** Monitoring heart rate can provide insights into cardiovascular health, activity levels, and potential arrhythmias.

- **Blood Pressure:** Continuous blood pressure monitoring can be crucial for managing hypertension and other cardiovascular conditions.
- **Sleep Patterns:** Tracking sleep duration and quality can help identify sleep disorders and improve overall health.
- **Activity Levels:** Monitoring steps taken, distance covered, and activity intensity can motivate individuals to lead healthier lifestyles.
- **Blood Oxygen Levels:** Pulse oximeters worn on the wrist can track blood oxygen levels, which can be important for certain medical conditions.

The Power of Remote Monitoring:

Remote monitoring platforms collect data from wearable devices and transmit it securely to healthcare providers. This allows for:

- **Early Detection of Issues:** Continuous monitoring can help detect potential health problems early on, enabling timely intervention and potentially preventing complications.
- **Improved Disease Management:** Remote monitoring allows for adjustments to treatment plans based on real-time patient data, leading to better disease management.
- **Reduced Hospital Readmissions:** By closely monitoring patients after discharge, remote monitoring can help prevent complications and reduce hospital readmission rates.
- **Enhanced Patient Engagement:** Real-time access to their health data empowers patients to take a more active role in managing their health.
- **Improved Care Accessibility:** Remote monitoring can extend specialist care to patients in remote locations or

those with mobility limitations.

Examples of Wearable Devices and Remote Monitoring in Action:

- A cardiac patient uses a smartwatch to monitor their heart rate and rhythm, allowing their doctor to detect potential problems remotely.
- A patient with diabetes uses a continuous glucose monitor to track their blood sugar levels in real-time, enabling adjustments to insulin dosage.
- An individual recovering from surgery wears a wearable device that monitors vital signs and activity levels, allowing healthcare providers to assess their progress remotely.

Challenges and Considerations:

- **Data Security and Privacy:** Ensuring the security and privacy of sensitive patient data collected from wearable devices is paramount. Robust security protocols and clear data governance practices are essential.
- **Data Overload and Alert Fatigue:** The constant stream of data from wearables can overwhelm healthcare providers. Effective filtering and prioritization of alerts are crucial.
- **Accuracy and Reliability:** The accuracy and reliability of wearable devices need to be continuously monitored and validated to ensure data integrity.
- **Limited Access and Affordability:** Unequal access to technology and the affordability of wearable devices can exacerbate healthcare disparities.

The Future of Wearable Devices and Remote Monitoring:

The future of healthcare is increasingly remote and patient-centric. Wearable devices and remote monitoring will continue to evolve in several ways:

- **Integration with AI and Machine Learning:** AI-powered algorithms can analyze data from wearables to identify trends, predict potential health risks, and personalize treatment plans.
- **Advanced Sensors and Capabilities:** Wearable devices will become more sophisticated, incorporating new sensors to monitor a wider range of health parameters.
- **Improved Battery Life and User Comfort:** Advancements in battery technology and device design will lead to longer-lasting and more comfortable wearables.

By addressing the challenges and harnessing the potential of wearable devices and remote monitoring, we can create a future of healthcare that is more proactive, personalized, and accessible for all. This technology has the potential to transform how we deliver care, empowering patients to take charge of their health and improving overall health outcomes.

Personalized Health Risk Assessment: Taking Charge of Your Health

Traditionally, health risk assessments have been a one-size-fits-all approach. However, with the rise of big data, machine learning, and advancements in medical science, personalized health risk assessments are emerging as a powerful tool for proactive health management.

What is a Personalized Health Risk Assessment (HRA)?

A personalized HRA goes beyond traditional questionnaires by considering a wider range of factors to create a more comprehensive picture of your individual health risks. It typically includes:

- **Demographic Information:** Age, gender, ethnicity, and family medical history.
- **Lifestyle Habits:** Diet, physical activity level, smoking status, and alcohol consumption.
- **Biometric Data:** Blood pressure, cholesterol levels, and blood sugar levels (if available).
- **Genetic Testing (Optional):** In some cases, genetic testing can be incorporated to identify potential hereditary risks.

Benefits of Personalized HRAs:

- **Early Detection of Risks:** By identifying potential health risks early, individuals can take preventive measures to reduce their chances of developing chronic diseases.
- **Personalized Risk Management:** HRAs provide insights into the specific health risks you face, allowing you to focus on areas that need the most attention.
- **Improved Health Awareness:** The process of completing an HRA can raise awareness about healthy behaviors and motivate individuals to adopt healthier lifestyles.
- **Empowerment and Action:** Personalized HRAs empower individuals to take charge of their health and make informed decisions about their well-being.

How Machine Learning Personalizes HRAs:

Machine learning algorithms can analyze vast datasets of health information to:

- **Identify Risk Factors:** Machine learning can identify subtle patterns in data that might be missed by traditional methods, leading to a more comprehensive understanding of individual risk factors.
- **Develop Predictive Models:** These models can predict the likelihood of developing specific diseases based on an individual's unique health profile.
- **Tailor Recommendations:** Based on the assessed risks, HRAs powered by machine learning can provide personalized recommendations for preventive measures and lifestyle changes.

Limitations and Considerations:

- **Data Accuracy:** The accuracy of an HRA relies on the accuracy of the data entered.
- **Not a Diagnosis:** An HRA is a screening tool, not a diagnostic test. It cannot definitively diagnose any medical condition.
- **Over-reliance on Technology:** HRAs should not replace regular checkups with a healthcare professional.
- **Access and Equity:** Unequal access to technology and digital literacy can limit the benefits of HRAs for certain populations.

The Future of Personalized HRAs:

The future of personalized HRAs is bright, with advancements in several areas:

- **Integration with Wearable Devices:** Data from wearable devices can be incorporated into HRAs, providing a more continuous and dynamic picture of an individual's health.
- **Advanced Risk Prediction Models:** Machine learning models will become more sophisticated, leading to more accurate risk predictions and personalized recommendations.
- **Actionable Insights and Gamification:** HRAs will move beyond simply providing information and will offer actionable steps and motivational tools to promote healthy behavior change.

By harnessing the power of data and machine learning, personalized HRAs can empower individuals to take a proactive approach to their health, fostering a future of preventive healthcare and improved overall well-being.

Important Note: While personalized HRAs offer valuable insights, they should not be used as a substitute for professional medical advice. Always consult with your doctor to discuss your health concerns and create a personalized healthcare plan.

CHAPTER TEN

DEEP LEARNING IN ACTION: REAL-WORLD EXAMPLES

eepMind, a subsidiary of Google focused on artificial intelligence research, has been at the forefront of developing AI for diabetic retinopathy (DR) detection. Their work centers around creating a prototype system to automate the screening and detection of DR using deep learning algorithms.

Here's a breakdown of DeepMind's approach to DR detection with AI:

- **Focus on Deep Learning:** Deep learning algorithms are a type of machine learning particularly adept at image recognition. DeepMind's system is trained on vast datasets of retinal images, allowing it to identify patterns associated with DR.
- **Prototype System:** DeepMind's creation is currently a prototype, meaning it's still under development and not

yet commercially available for widespread use in clinical settings.

- **Multi-Disease Detection:** While the primary focus seems to be on DR, some reports suggest the system might be capable of detecting other retinal diseases like glaucoma and age-related macular degeneration (AMD).

Potential Benefits:

- **Improved Screening Efficiency:** AI-powered systems have the potential to analyze retinal images much faster than human specialists, potentially reducing screening backlogs and allowing for earlier detection of DR.
- **Reduced Costs:** Automating DR screening could potentially lead to cost savings in the healthcare system.
- **Increased Accessibility:** AI-based systems could be deployed in remote locations or areas with limited access to ophthalmologists, improving access to DR screening for a wider population.

Important Considerations:

- **Regulatory Approval:** DeepMind's AI system for DR detection is not yet approved by regulatory bodies like the FDA in the US. This is crucial before widespread clinical use.
- **Explainability and Transparency:** Deep learning models can be complex, and ensuring the transparency and explainability of the AI's decision-making process is vital for trust and adoption in healthcare.
- **Data Bias:** The AI system's performance is highly dependent on the data it's trained on. Mitigating bias in the training data is crucial to ensure accurate and fair

detection across diverse patient populations.

The Current Landscape:

DeepMind's project is one of several ongoing efforts to leverage AI for DR detection. While promising, it's important to remember that AI is not meant to replace ophthalmologists entirely. Rather, it can be a valuable tool to assist healthcare professionals in screening and early detection of DR, potentially leading to better patient outcomes.

Freenome is a company at the forefront of utilizing deep learning for early cancer detection through what they call a multiomics platform. Here's a deeper dive into Freenome's approach and its potential impact:

Freenome's Approach:

- **Multiomics Platform:** Unlike some approaches that focus on analyzing genetic mutations, Freenome's platform takes a broader look. It analyzes various biological data points, including:

  - **DNA methylation:** Chemical modifications to DNA that can influence gene expression.
  - **Gene expression:** The level of activity of different genes.
  - **Protein levels:** The abundance of various proteins in the blood.
  - **Microbiome:** The community of microbes living in the gut.

- **Deep Learning Analysis:**Freenome leverages deep learning algorithms to analyze this vast amount of multiomics data from a simple blood draw. The algorithms are trained to identify subtle patterns associated with the presence of cancer, even in its early stages.

- **Focus on Multiple Cancers:**Freenome is developing tests for the early detection of various cancers, with a current focus on colorectal cancer and lung cancer.

Potential Benefits:

- **Early Detection:**Freenome's blood test has the potential to detect cancer earlier than traditional methods, leading to better treatment outcomes and potentially saving lives.
- **Non-invasive Approach:** A simple blood test offers a more convenient and less invasive alternative to some traditional cancer screening methods.
- **Improved Screening Rates:** A blood test might encourage more people to undergo cancer screening, leading to earlier detection across the population.

Challenges and Considerations:

- **Validation and Regulatory Approval:** Freenome's tests are still under development and require further validation through clinical trials. Regulatory approval from bodies like the FDA is necessary before widespread clinical use.
- **Specificity and Accuracy:** Ensuring the accuracy of the test and minimizing false positives (incorrectly indicating cancer) is crucial.
- **Data Privacy and Security:** Protecting patients' sensitive health data is paramount. Robust security measures and clear data governance practices are

essential.

The Future of Freenome's Technology:
Freenome's approach holds promise for revolutionizing early cancer detection. Here's a glimpse into the future:

- **Expansion to More Cancers:**Freenome's platform could be adapted to detect a wider range of cancers in the future.
- **Integration with Other Technologies:**Freenome's tests could be combined with other technologies like wearable devices for a more comprehensive picture of an individual's health.
- **Personalized Risk Assessment:** The multiomics data might be used to develop personalized risk assessments for different types of cancer.

By overcoming the challenges and continuing to refine their technology, Freenome has the potential to significantly improve early cancer detection rates, leading to a future where cancer is diagnosed and treated at its earliest stages.

Enlitic: Empowering Healthcare with AI-powered Medical Image Analysis

Enlitic is a medical technology company at the forefront of applying artificial intelligence (AI) to revolutionize medical image analysis. Their AI platform offers a comprehensive suite of solutions designed to improve workflow efficiency, enhance diagnostic accuracy, and unlock the potential of medical imaging data.

Enlitic's AI Solutions:

- **ENDEX:** This data standardization solution tackles the challenge of inconsistencies and complexities often plaguing medical imaging data. By standardizing images, ENDEX streamlines workflows, improves data quality, and facilitates better analysis.
- **ENCOG™:** This intelligent solution addresses patient privacy concerns in medical image analysis. ENCOG leverages AI to de-identify images while preserving clinically relevant information. This enables secure data sharing and analysis for research and development purposes.
- **Ensight:** This is Enlitic's core platform, an extensible framework that integrates various AI-powered applications for medical image analysis. Ensight facilitates the deployment, management, and orchestration of these applications, allowing healthcare institutions to tailor solutions to their specific needs.

Benefits of Enlitic's AI Platform:

- **Improved Workflow Efficiency:** Standardized data and automated analysis tools can significantly reduce processing time and streamline workflows for radiologists and other healthcare professionals.
- **Enhanced Diagnostic Accuracy:** AI algorithms can assist radiologists in identifying subtle abnormalities and potential disease patterns, potentially leading to more accurate diagnoses.
- **Advanced Research and Development:** Secure data sharing through ENCOG empowers researchers to leverage vast datasets for medical image analysis, accelerating advancements in diagnosis and treatment.

- **Data-Driven Insights:**Enlitic's platform allows healthcare institutions to unlock the value of their medical imaging data, gaining insights into patient populations and improving overall healthcare delivery.

Examples of Enlitic's Impact:

- A large hospital system utilizes ENDEX to standardize its medical imaging data archive, enabling faster retrieval and analysis of patient information.
- A research consortium leverages ENCOG to securely share de-identified medical images for a large-scale study on a specific disease.
- A radiology department integrates Ensight with their existing workflow, utilizing AI for preliminary analysis and flagging potential abnormalities for radiologist review.

Challenges and Considerations:

- **Regulatory Landscape:** As with any AI-powered medical technology, navigating regulatory requirements and ensuring compliance is crucial.
- **Algorithmic Bias:**Enlitic's AI models need to be trained on high-quality, diverse datasets to mitigate bias and ensure fair and accurate results across patient populations.
- **Integration and Interoperability:** Seamless integration of Enlitic's platform with existing healthcare IT systems is essential for widespread adoption.

The Future of Enlitic's Technology:

Enlitic is continuously innovating and evolving its AI platform. Here's a glimpse into the future:

- **Expansion of AI Applications:**Enlitic is likely to develop and integrate new AI applications for analyzing a wider range of medical images and assisting with various diagnostic tasks.
- **Focus on Explainable AI:** Developing AI models that are more transparent and provide clear explanations for their decisions will be crucial for building trust in AI-powered diagnostics.
- **Cloud-based Solutions:** Cloud-based deployment of Enlitic's platform could increase accessibility and scalability for healthcare institutions.

By addressing the challenges and continuing to develop their AI platform, Enlitic has the potential to significantly transform medical image analysis, leading to a future of more efficient workflows, improved diagnostic accuracy, and ultimately, better patient care.

CHAPTER ELEVEN

CONCLUSION

Deep learning, a powerful subset of artificial intelligence, is rapidly transforming the healthcare landscape. By unlocking the potential of vast amounts of medical data, deep learning offers a multitude of benefits for patients, healthcare providers, and the future of medicine itself.

Revolutionizing Clinical Trials: Deep learning can optimize clinical trial design by streamlining patient recruitment, leveraging real-world data, and enabling more efficient trial structures. This can expedite drug development, reduce costs, and ultimately deliver life-saving treatments faster.

Empowering Personalized Medicine: Deep learning empowers personalized medicine by analyzing an individual's unique genetic makeup, phenotypic data, and real-time health information. This allows for tailored preventive measures, more effective treatment selection, and optimized medication dosages, leading to improved patient outcomes.

Transforming Patient Engagement: Virtual assistants and chatbots powered by deep learning empower patients by providing 24/7 access to information, appointment scheduling tools, and personalized guidance. This fosters a more proactive approach to health management and improves the overall patient experience.

Enhancing Remote Monitoring: Wearable devices and remote monitoring platforms powered by deep learning allow healthcare professionals to continuously track patient health data outside the clinical setting. This enables early detection of health issues, improved disease management, and empowers patients to take charge of their health.

Personalized Health Risk Assessment: Deep learning personalizes health risk assessments by incorporating a wider range of factors and leveraging vast datasets to identify potential health risks. This allows for early intervention and preventive measures, promoting a future of proactive healthcare.

Early Disease Detection: DeepMind's AI for diabetic retinopathy detection and Freenome's multiomics platform for early cancer screening are just a few examples of how deep learning is revolutionizing disease detection. These advancements have the potential to save lives through earlier intervention and improved treatment outcomes.

Empowering Healthcare Professionals: Enlitic's AI platform for medical image analysis exemplifies how deep learning can assist healthcare professionals. By streamlining workflows, enhancing diagnostic accuracy, and facilitating research, AI empowers healthcare professionals to deliver better care.

Challenges and the Road Ahead:

While the potential of deep learning in healthcare is vast, challenges remain, including data privacy and security, regulatory considerations, algorithmic bias, and ensuring equitable access to these technologies. Addressing these challenges and fostering responsible development are crucial to ensure deep learning fulfills its promise.

A Future of Personalized, Proactive Healthcare:

Deep learning represents a paradigm shift in healthcare, paving the way for a future of personalized, data-driven medicine. Imagine a future where preventive measures are tailored to your unique needs, treatments are optimized for your specific biology, and you are empowered to actively participate in your own health journey. This is the future that deep learning in healthcare promises to unlock.

By harnessing the power of deep learning and fostering responsible innovation, we can create a healthcare system that is more efficient, effective, and empowering for all.

CHAPTER TWELVE

REFERENCES

1. Precision Medicine Initiative (NIH). https://www.nih.gov/precision-medicine-initiative-cohort-program (12 November 2016, date last accessed).

2. Collins FS, Varmus H.. A new initiative on precision medicine. *N Engl J Med* 2015;372:793–5.

3. Miotto R, Weng C.. Case-based reasoning using electronic health records efficiently identifies eligible patients for clinical trials. *J Am Med Inform Assoc* 2015;22:e141–50.

4. Libbrecht MW, Noble WS.. Machine learning applications in genetics and genomics. *Nat Rev Genet* 2015;16:321–32.

5. Hripcsak G, Albers DJ.. Next-generation phenotyping of electronic health records. *J Am Med Inform Assoc* 2013;20:117–21. [PMC free article] [PubMed]

6. LeCun Y, Bengio Y, Hinton G.. Deep learning. *Nature* 2015;521:436–44.

7. Liu C, Wang F, Hu J, *et al.* Risk prediction with electronic health records: a deep learning approach. In: *ACM International Conference on Knowledge Discovery and Data Mining*, Sydney, NSW, Australia, 2015, 705–14.

8. Liang Z, Zhang G, Huang JX, *et al.* Deep learning for healthcare decision making with EMRs. In IEEE

International Conference on Bioinformatics and Biomedicine, 2014, 556–9.

9. Jindal V, Birjandtalab J, Pouyan MB, *et al.* An adaptive deep learning approach for PPG-based identification. In: *38th Annual International Conference of the IEEE Engineering in Medicine and Biology Society (EMBC)*, Orlando, FL, USA, 2016, 6401–4.

10. Mamoshina P, Vieira A, Putin E, *et al.* Applications of deep learning in biomedicine. *Mol Pharm* 2016;13:1445–54.

11. Angermueller C, Pärnamaa T, Parts L, *et al.* Deep learning for computational biology. *Mol Syst Biol* 2016;12:878.

12. Park Y, Kellis M.. Deep learning for regulatory genomics. *Nat Biotechnol* 2015;33:825–6.

13. LeCun Y, Bengio Y, Hinton G (2015) Deep learning. Nature 521(7553):436–444. https://doi.org/10.1038/nature14539

14. Fu Y, Lei Y, Wang T, Curran WJ, Liu T, Yang X (2020) Deep learning in medical image registration: a review. Phys Med Biol 65(20). https://doi.org/10.1088/1361-6560/ab843e

15. Haskins G, Kruger U, Yan P (2020) Deep learning in medical image registration: a survey. Mach Vis Appl 31:1–18. https://doi.org/10.1007/s00138-020-01060-x

16. Shen D, Wu G, Suk H (2017) Deep learning in medical image analysis. Annu Rev Biomed Eng 19:221–248. https://doi.org/10.1146/annurev-bioeng-071516-044442

17. D. Ravi, *et al.* Deep learning for health informaticsIEEE J. Biomed. Heal. Informatics, 21 (1) (2017), pp. 4-21, 10.1109/JBHI.2016.2636665

18. Chang, *et al.* A deep learning-based intelligent medicine recognition system for chronic patientsIEEE

Access, 7 (2019), pp. 44441-44458

19. Andre Esteva, *et al.*A guide to deep learning in healthcareNat Med, 25 (Jan 2019), pp. 24-29

20. Rui Zhao, *et al.*Deep learning and its applications to machine health monitoring: a surveyMech Syst Signal Process, 14 (No. 8) (Aug 2015)

CHAPTER THIRTEEN

ABOUT AUTHORS

Mrs. S.FOWJIYA, an eminent academician, currently serving as Assistant Professor in the Department of Computer science and Technology at Vivekanandha College of Engineering for Women (Autonomous), Elayampalayam, Tiruchengode, Namakkal Dt. She is presently pursuing Ph.D. in Anna University under the domain Deep learning. Her research focuses mainly on Medical data. Her research title is "An Efficient approach for an Early Prognosis of Preeclampsia and its Feasible Risks Using Hybrid Neural Networks" under the guidance of Dr.T. Abirami, ASP/IT, Kongu Engineering College,Perundurai. She is graduated with a Master's degree (M.E -CCE) from Tamilnadu College of Engineering and Technology in 2013 and Bachelor's degree (B.Tech -IT) from Vivekanandha Institute of Engineering and Technology for women in 2011. She has six years of expertise in teaching, research, administration, and academia. She was awarded with the Best Faculty 2023 and Best Faculty 2024 Consecutively from VCEW. She is a certified Mentor and AI Coach for Youth program in India by DELL Technologies and Intel Digital Readiness.Her Commitment towards the Profession and research contributions are commendable, with numerous papers published in prestigious international and national journals. As a highly regarded expert in her field, she actively evaluates UG projects and hackathons .Her fondness in teaching nurture many young minds through various Experiential Learning methods. Her mastery spans covers wide range of subjects, like Artificial Intelligence, Datascience, Machine Learning , Internet of Things (IoT), Design Thinking ,Operating systems, Data Structures, ,C and C++, Python, JAVA ,OSS.She earned a higher number of participation certificates in Online Webinar, Workshop, Faculty Development Program and Hands on Training. She has been honored with several well-earned honors and prizes during her career.

Mrs.S. BRINDHA is a dedicated professional with a passion for education. She holds a M.E degree in Computer Science and Engineering, M.B.A degree in Software Enterprises Management and a B.E degree in Computer Science and Engineering. She is currently working as an Assistant Professor at Vivekanandha College of Engineering for Women (Autonomous), Elayampalayam, Tiruchengode, Namakkal (Dt). She has actively participated in workshops, and Seminars, Webinar and Faculty Development Program in both National and International levels and also she has published one paper in the Conference. She is having interest in the research area of Machine Learning, Deep Learning, Artificial Intelligence and Big data. She has published one book under the title of "Machine Learning for Healthcare Informatics: Extracting Valuable Insights from Big Data" in the month of November 2023. She has produced 100% results in UG and PG subjects.

Ms. P. SUDHA is a dedicated professional with a passion for education. She holds a M.E degree in Computer Science and Engineering from Gnanamani College of Technology, Namakkal and a B.E degree in Computer Science and Engineering from Gnanamani College of Engineering, Namakkal. Currently working as an Assistant Professor at Vivekanandha College of Engineering for Women (Autonomous), Elayampalayam, Tiruchengode, Namakkal. She has one year of teaching involvement with reputed organizations. She has actively participated in workshops, and seminars, Webinar and Faculty Development Program in both National and International levels. She presented paper at international conferences in India. She produced 100% Results in Academic year 2023-2024.She received certificates from ICT Academy, Cisco Networking Academy and NPTEL Certificates.Her area of interest is Computer Networks, Operating Systems, Data Structures, Machine Learning, Artificial Intelligence, Internet of Things (IoT), web designing, Programming languages like C, C++ , Python and etc.,